COLOR

GUIDE TO BULBS &

ANNUALS

COLOR

GUIDE TO BULBS &

ANNUALS

Keran Barrett & Helen Moody

bay books

CONTENTS

INTRODUCTION TO

BULBS & ANNUALS

Like interior design, gardening is subject to fashion and fads, with particular types of plants going in and out of favor. And although annuals and bulbs have had their peaks and troughs, they are still fashionable, accessible, and easy to grow, satisfying the time-poor, novice or addicted gardener.

In Victorian England, annuals were a garden favorite. Neat, box-hedged, geometric parterres and knot gardens were filled with seasonal annuals, and carpet bedding was all the rage. At various times, large estates and municipal parks and gardens have been carefully designed into formal bedding schemes, usually very brightly colored, often in contrasting hues, and laid out in patterns or planted in borders in slightly more informal blocks of color. Imitating these styles, home gardeners have also used annuals more informally, creating color highlights among bulbs, perennials or shrubs, or mixing them all. Annuals can be planted in drifts, as fillers, edging or as color blocks, and featured in meadow or wildflower gardens. Their uses are endless.

In this design, pansies are contained by a zig-zag planting of box hedges, a traditional favorite in formal schemes.

Bulbs have never really gone out of favor, but with the exception of a handful that have attracted enormous interest, they've often been overlooked or been considered too specialized. The phenomenon of "Tulipmania" that swept Holland in the 16th century has never really subsided, although the once astronomical prices paid for these bulbs have been replaced by far more realistic and affordable ones today! Along with daffodils, crocus, and hyacinth, tulips continue to be one of the "fab four" favorites; they are used extensively in gardens, parks, and festivals during spring, but there are many more that deserve far greater attention just waiting to be explored. Elizabeth Lawrence, the garden writer, wrote of *Crocus pulchellus* (*pulchellus* meaning pretty): "Well named, for the flowers are so adorable that it is hard to describe them without sounding foolish." The same could be said for many other bulbs.

Fluted, recurved petals give these gloriosa lilies an airy, floating effect.

GARDENING TODAY

Around the world there is a trend towards smaller gardens and less leisure time. So when it comes to gardening, people want low-maintenance courtyards, patios, and gardens, which means more hard surfaces, fewer garden beds, and more permanent plantings. Annuals are perfect for "compact living," whether for small spaces or containers: they're small, quick to flower, and come in almost every shade, hue, and form. And if you are time-poor, annuals can be a help rather than a hindrance, as they don't need pruning or pampering—simply pull them out at the end of the season and replace them with another color or design. Bulbs offer exquisite and interesting flowers, perfect for enjoying in a confined space, such as a courtyard. Many will multiply, producing more plants and more blooms year after year, with very little effort on your part.

Nurseries around the world are catering for this trend for "instant" gardens, finding new ways of making annuals popular. There are semi-advanced seedlings sold in larger cell packs, already with some in flower; there are pots of mature plants sold as "potted color," "bloomers," and "mixed containers," and hanging baskets that have already been planted. Bulbs that are commonly enjoyed for indoor flowering displays are "prepared" by growers, so all you need to do is take them home.

Here, the pinks of schizanthus, tulips and kale are complemented by the blue flowers of lobelia.

As we write this book, widespread regions in both the United States and Australia have experienced severe drought and tight water restrictions, ongoing in many areas, and recently Europe had its hottest summer on record. Yes, many annuals and bulbs do need regular watering during their growing periods, but there are many products that reduce the watering requirements of all plants on the market these days. There are also annuals and bulbs that are drought tolerant, or at least dry tolerant. Since bulbs often need a dry dormancy, water is of little concern during this period—unlike perennials or shrubs, which need more constant moisture.

Modern breeding and production techniques are creating ever more attractive annuals, with newer cultivars being more compact, uniform or reliable. The popularity of the new cutting-produced plants, such as annual surfinas, is driving the demand for premium products. Pedigreed, highly bred annuals, with better garden performance and improved disease resistance—such as giant pansies and spreading petunias—are best sellers around the world. And with breeding programs expanding into the world of bulbs, not only are there bigger, brighter, more reliable favorites, but also available are different varieties that can be grown outside their normal climate, making them accessible to a wider gardening audience.

California poppies thrive in hot, dry conditions.

WHAT ARE ANNUALS AND BULBS?

It's generally accepted that an annual is a plant that germinates from seed, grows, sets seed, and dies within a year. Biennials germinate in their first year, produce leaves in their first season, then flower, set seed, and die in their second. Perennials are plants that live for a number of years without becoming woody with age, unlike trees and shrubs.

There are many genera where there are distinct annual, biennial, and perennial species, but varying climatic conditions, the development of new cultivars, and new uses for specific flowers have blurred the distinctions among annuals, biennials, and short-lived perennials, and many new plants don't conform to the rules.

With modern plant breeders deliberately producing plants that will flower more quickly, what was once a perennial is now manipulated and designed to be an annual. There are also some longer lived perennials that need a winter chilling, so these can only be grown as annuals in warmer climates. Conversely, some plants may behave as annuals in a cold climate, where the onset of cold winter temperatures, particularly frost, will kill them; but when grown in a warm temperate climate, they may well overwinter for a year, perhaps two.

Allium and aquilegia are charming additions to a cottage garden.

So what about bulbs? These days, through nurseries and mail order catalogs, suppliers will often promote plants that aren't strictly bulbs, so we have avoided the purist approach and have included all "types" in this book. The term "bulb" is frequently applied to a range of plants with some kind of underground storage organ, including true bulbs, corms, tubers, tuberous roots, rhizomes, and pseudobulbs.

As with annuals, climate affects the performance of bulbs. They are usually treated as perennials but in some locations perform like annuals, and falling into "warm-climate" or "cold-climate" groups, their origins will determine their suitability for your location.

We discuss climate and bulb types in more detail in the "Reference" section and have signposted some of the anomalies or specific requirements in our individual A to Z plant entries. But if you are uncertain you should refer to the information on seed packets or seedling labels, which are generally climate specific, and to the bulb packs or cultural information leaflets that may accompany them.

Select annuals and bulbs according to their natural growing requirements, or 'force' hyacinths and other bulbs to grow out of season.

LANDSCAPING: USING COLOR

Color affects your mood, reflects your personality, and if used with care, brings harmony to your environment. Color also dramatically impacts on the style and mood of gardens. With annuals in particular being so colorful, it can be easy to end up with a "riot" happening in your garden beds instead of the calming or bold effect you're striving for, but if you follow some simple guidelines, the results can be stunning.

The color wheel

As most colors are blends of each other, they are organized in a "wheel" rather than on a straight line. All colors are created from the three primary or true colors of red, blue, and yellow. Secondary colors are equal blends of primary colors—for example, orange (red/yellow), green (blue/yellow), and violet (red/blue). Hues and tones, or tertiary colors, are an imbalance created by mixing a primary and a secondary color from the same part of the wheel.

Contrasting colors are those opposite each other on the color wheel. They make a bold and dramatic statement when planted side by side. Try these combinations—orange (warm) and blue (cool), yellow (warm) and violet (cool), or red (warm) and green (cool). Use one as a dominant color, the other to offset it.

Complementary colors, however, are those closest to each other on the color wheel. They harmonize with each other—think red, orange, and yellow—and they'll never clash or conflict visually.

For maximum impact, use flowers in contrasting colors, such as yellow gazanias and purple-pink verbena.

To help you design a garden incorporating, or based on, annuals and bulbs, the plants featured in this book have been classified according to color. As well as a mixed color display, consider designing a monochromatic garden, using various hues and shades of a single color through flowers and foliage.

Multicolors

Plants don't always fall neatly into a category, especially when they're available in an array of colors and shades—as well as blotches, stripes, and two-tones. These are often best planted en masse rather than mixed with many different types of plants, so the plant variety itself provides consistency. Alternatively, add one other color to draw the whole scene together, perhaps the most dominant color, soft pastels or white.

Warm

Red, orange, and yellow are happy and cheerful colors that tend to visually come towards you, creating an air of intimacy, great for "reducing" the size of a large garden. Many tropical plants bloom in these colors, so while you may not have that type of climate, imitation is a way of living "hot." To lower the temperature of a warm design, add a little cool color; the key is the subtlety of the addition, not equal balance.

Cool

Light shades of cool colors such as blue and green recede, providing an impression of space. So to make a small area look larger, add cool colors near the back of the garden. Add a few warm tones to heat up a

These blowzy, burgundy-colored tulips demand attention.

predominantly cool color scheme. In tropical or warm climates or in the heat of summer, these calming colors bring a sense of respite, and relief from the heat. Green accompanies any design, particularly if swathes of foliage provide a backdrop to the rest of the garden.

Pink

Created by blending varying degrees of warm red with cool blue, depending on the shade or tone, pink can be shocking or shy. You can use pinks in either a warm or cool color scheme. However, soft pinks are often better suited to a pastel design, while bolder shades, such as cerise, create a dramatic effect when matched with rich purples or dark blues. Experiment, and explore combinations that you find appealing.

White

White is the gardener's friend. As it is neutral, it can be incorporated into a warm scheme to tone it down, or into a cool scheme to add crisp overtones. White is versatile, accompanying and enhancing every color of the rainbow; it is also a favorite stand-alone display. Glowing at night, white flowers planted close to the house provide some natural illumination. And they are the obvious choice for weddings.

Pastel

White with a touch of color, or is it vice versa? Adding white to any color produces gentle shades of cream, apricot, pink, blue, lavender, and lime green—a soft partnership in any garden theme that sits comfortably with both warm and cool colors. Pastels produce a whisper, not a shout.

Use white on its own, or accompany it with pastels or silver; intersperse it with strong colors to show off its purity.

Although silver and gray are not "true" colors, they provide the perfect foliage accompaniment for many color schemes by enhancing colors or toning them down.

Using bulbs and annuals

Color is all about personal choice and experimentation, but it works better if you try to harmonize the colors of the house, fence, and paving with the garden. The next time you select flower shades at the nursery, take along some paint swatches to help you.

Annuals (and biennials) are the quickest and most economical way of bringing color and life to gardens, patios, and balconies. They offer variety and the chance to change the look of the garden from one season to another. They also enable you to experiment with color schemes and signal seasonal changes.

Annuals can be used in many different ways—as temporary fillers in new gardens, as fillers between trees and shrubs until they mature, or as color experiments before you decide on perennials and shrubs. They can be grown in pots, troughs, and hanging baskets, and used to fill in bare patches in mixed borders, providing ever-changing interest. They are also an indispensable component of the cottage garden, with its informal planting style. Plant annuals along with bulbs, in clumps or drifts or as edging, or mixed with perennials and shrubs to produce a more natural look than the rather old-fashioned idea of bedding annuals displayed on their own.

This color scheme has red as its foundation. Experiment, change the mood with annuals until you're satisfied—and enjoy.

When planting bulbs and annuals in a border, try to avoid a jumble of plants, too close together, with taller ones hiding smaller ones and colors clashing. Take the time to plan your border carefully by looking at flower color and plant shape, height, and spread, aiming for a mix of tall, spreading, spiky, and mounded plants. Plant irregular, odd-numbered groups rather than individual plants in plain, straight lines.

Place taller plants at the back if your border is to be viewed only from the front, then graduate down to lower growing and spilling plants at the front. Incorporate the odd group of taller plants towards the front to break up the line. If the border is to be viewed from both sides, place taller plants in the center, reducing the height towards either end. A good technic for drawing a planting scheme together is to repeat groups of the same plants along the length of the border.

Container planting

One of the best things about growing annuals in pots and hanging baskets is that you can experiment with color schemes and the following year do it all over again, coming up with another theme that will change the personality of your patio, courtyard, balcony or garden. Containers are also useful for bulbs that die down during their dormant season, as these can be tucked out of sight and later brought back into prominence to display their blooms. Alternatively, bury the container in a garden bed to disguise it and restrict any wandering habits.

Cool and calming blues, white, and pinks. Select low-growing varieties for the front of the border and add height at the back.

Today, there's an enormous array of pots, urns, planters, hanging or wall baskets available, made from materials ranging from plastic imitation-terracotta to the real thing, ceramic, colored glass or metals. Containers may be free standing (perfect as portable gardens) or custom built into a landscape design—ideal for those with limited space. And be selective when buying pots—don't end up with one of everything, or limit yourself to the black nursery pots. Choose colors, styles, and designs that suit your environment and the plants that will fill them. Place pots together in groups for focal points, because single containers, unless they are very large or ornate, can look lost. Don't forget to hang baskets at eye level where you can enjoy and reach them. Soften container edges with spill-over plants and incorporate fragrant plants in pots near seating and windows.

For massed planting displays, choose large containers and group those with the same watering and sun requirements together. Remember, small pots dry out faster, creating more work and using more water. Always buy the best planting mix blended for containers or bulbs, as these normally contain water-storing granules and extra nutrients. So select thoughtfully, plant smartly, and you'll never look back.

Fill small spaces with color by planting in containers. Many annuals, such as pansies, come in an array of colors to suit any design.

WHAT'S IN THIS BOOK?

We've compiled a collection of favorites and plants for specific purposes, plus some less familiar plants that are popular with those who grow them. This selection of annuals and bulbs isn't meant to be definitive; it's simply a guide to some of the best known, the most widely available, and those worth seeking out. You will no doubt find others in nurseries and particularly in mail order or Internet catalogs—more obscure and rarer plants, unusual forms, choicer or more challenging species. If our selection gives you a guide, and whets your appetite for more, we have done our job.

Why not wander around your neighbourhood, visit large parks, spring festivals, and open gardens to gather further inspiration? Seek information from local nurseries and specialist growers as well as catalog suppliers. Don't be afraid to ask for advice and talk with other gardeners—and to experiment. Gardening should be all about having fun and having a go. You never know what joys and green thumbs it may yield!

Note

In this book we have used The Royal Horticultural Society references as the final arbiters for some glossary definitions, and we have usually used it whenever we have found contradictory botanical information.

Color schemes can be subtle or bold. Why not visit open gardens for some ideas?

MULTICOLORS

A re you crazy about colors? Tempted by two-tones? Are you bedazzled by bicolors? If you want it all, then the multicolors are for you! Either growing naturally or bred through modern hybridization techniques, the plants in this chapter may produce several exquisite shades and tones on one flower. As if created by an exuberant artist, the palette of color is endless.

Often blooming in every color of the rainbow, with no one shade predominating, this selection of plants refuses to be labeled. Multicolors offer choice: pick a single color and choose the flowers that suit your scheme. Look for crimson, maroon, deep blue, bright yellow, amber or pink—within this chapter you're bound to find the perfect hue for your color scheme.

If you're indecisive about colors, then choose them all. Avoid a "riot of color" by planting the same type of flower: its form provides uniformity, allowing you to use a wider selection of colors, tones, and hues. Stripes and speckles sit comfortably with single colors. Synergy is created with mass planting, fusing colors or separating them. Select your desired composition, experiment, and enjoy.

ALCEA ROSEA
HOLLYHOCK

Hollyhocks have been cultivated in England since the 16th century, but the exact Middle Eastern origins and original forms of these dramatic plants have been lost in time. Today's hollyhock spikes bear single, double or semidouble flowers in many shades of pink, cranberry, purple, apricot, yellow, white, and nearly black. Although still a popular component of the cottage garden, the towering 10 ft (3 m) spires are best used as background plants close to walls or fences where they can be tied or staked. Even dwarf varieties such as those in the Majorette Group grow to 3 ft (90 cm). Sometimes classified as a perennial or hardy biennial, hollyhocks are commonly grown as an annual to flower in their first year. The flowers open in progression, from the bottom up, through summer to early fall.

Tall and stately, hollyhock flowers come in almost all colors except blue.

GROWING NOTES

Suited to all but a tropical climate, hollyhocks grown as annuals in a cold climate are best sown in a greenhouse. Plants need fertilizer and plenty of water during the growing season. They are vulnerable to attack by rust diseases, so avoid growing them in the same spot for more than one or two years.

ANEMONE CORONARIA
WINDFLOWER

Saying farewell to winter and hello to a new spring and summer are the flamboyant poppy-like *Anemone coronaria* of the Mediterranean. The most popular are the De Caen Group—blooming with single flowers in white, bright pink, red or purple—and the St. Brigid Group, going one step further by displaying semidouble or double flowers in bright colors, pastels or bicolors. Other cultivars are also available. Similar to ranunculus, their cheerful relatives, anemones are distinguished by the ruffle of leaves beneath their flowers. Plant them in borders and pots.

Perfect for cutting, anemones are also known as the florist's poppy.

GROWING NOTES

Anemones enjoy cold, cool, and warm climates in a frost-free, sunny or partially shady spot. Plant them with the pointy end of the corm facing down at a depth of 1½ in (4 cm) during fall or winter, with a spacing of 4 in (10 cm) between each. In areas prone to wet or very cold winters, plant in spring. Anemones prefer well-drained, friable soil; add lime if your soil is acid. Treat corms as annuals, replacing them each year, as they lose vigor with age.

BEGONIA X SEMPERFLORENS-CULTORUM
WAX BEGONIA

The waxy flowers of *Begonia* x *semperflorens-cultorum* blend well together and with other plants in the garden.

Not every plant can hold center stage, and if ever there were one ideally suited for the chorus line, then wax begonia must be it. These unobtrusive but easy-care plants blend so well into gardens that you'll find them in parterres and formal bedding schemes, as edging plants, and in window boxes, troughs, and pots. Neat and compact, they will grow in sun or part shade to provide color from late spring until frost. The slightly succulent stems and shiny bronze or green leaves become smothered in small, waxy single or double flowers in many shades of red, pink, and white. In cold areas they can be moved indoors for winter.

GROWING NOTES

Bedding begonias adapt to most climates, even tolerating hot humid conditions. Wax begonia seed is sown in spring to early summer and needs light for germination. These plants can also be propagated from cuttings. Tubers can be lifted in the fall and stored dry.

BEGONIA TUBERHYBRIDA
TUBEROUS BEGONIA

In contrast to wax begonia, tuberous begonia hybrids are ideal candidates for a starring role. There are both upright and pendulous types, and their large and often gorgeously frilled or ruffled single or double flowers come in almost every color except blue, many with pretty picotee edging. They are popular florist lines and are often displayed in public conservatories. Once tuberous begonias were largely limited to specialist growers, but there are now seed-raised varieties that flower quickly to perform as annuals. With their bright, clear colors and beautiful blooms, they make stunning container flowers as well as bedding plants.

GROWING NOTES

Tuberous begonias do best where summers are cool and moist. For best results grow them in damp, rich, well-drained soil with lots of added organic matter. They prefer morning sun or dappled shade, but will become a little leggy and thin-stemmed in heavy shade.

Above: Tuberous begonias have large ruffled flowers in a wide range of colors, many with picotee edging like this one.

Opposite: *B. tuberhybrida* Non Stop Series 'Orange'.

BRACTEANTHA BRACTEATA
SYN. *HELICHRYSUM BRACTEATUM*

STRAWFLOWER

From the fields and forests of their native land to the hanging baskets of Europe and North America, these Australian plants are botanically fascinating. Their daisy-like flower heads are made up of papery bracts in clear, bright shades of gold, bronze, russet, and red, plus cream and soft pink. Planted in pockets in rock gardens or massed in wildflower gardens, *Bracteantha* attract birds and squirrels. They perform to perfection in pots, can be used as bedding, and are sold as fresh and dried cut flowers. There are tall varieties to 3 ft (1 m), and low-growing forms, most with gray-green foliage.

The papery flower heads of Australian everlasting or paper daisies make them excellent for dried flower arrangements.

GROWING NOTES

Grown as annuals or short-lived perennials in warmer climates, these sun-loving plants need a warm site and well-drained soil with average fertility. As strawflowers are natives of dry places, go easy on the water, as high humidity or continual damp may cause stem rot. Tip pruning and removing spent flowers will benefit them greatly. Harvest flowers for drying before they open fully, and hang them upside down in a cool, dark place.

CALLISTEPHUS CHINENSIS
ASTER

Cultivated in China for over 2000 years, asters were lovingly depicted in ancient Chinese paintings. Once the early 18th century plant hunters took seed to Europe and the breeders started work, it was inevitable that asters would become worldwide favorites. The blue, pink, white, red, and purple flowers—often with yellow centers—that we grow today probably only faintly resemble the original. There are single and double blooms, shaggy, pompon, daisy-, chrysanthemum-, and peony-like flower heads, as well as tall and dwarf types. Although several strains have been bred for bedding and borders, asters are perhaps best known as floristry cut flowers.

Best known as floristry flowers, asters (sometimes called China asters) can look stunning in garden beds and borders.

GROWING NOTES
Asters are frost tender, so in cold climates sow seed in a greenhouse or *in situ* in warmer locations. They like a sunny site, sheltered from wind, with fertile, moist, well-drained neutral to alkaline soil; they also like to be well watered and mulched in dry weather. Asters are prone to wilt disease, so avoid planting them in the same location for more than one year at a time.

CHRYSANTHEMUM CORONARIUM;
C. CARINATUM SYN. C. TRICOLOR

PAINTED DAISY

The cultivar names 'Painted Daisy' and 'Monarch Court Jesters' vividly describe the annual *Chrysanthemum carinatum* (syn. *C. tricolor*). Their 3 in (8 cm) wide flowers have bands of yellow, red, and orange or scarlet, maroon, and white that are as colorful as the souks or marketplaces of their native Morocco. Tall and dwarf cultivars are available, and they are as easy to grow as they are colorful, making them a great choice for a child's garden. *C. coronarium*, the garland chrysanthemum, is a bushy annual species of Mediterranean origin. It grows to 3 ft (1 m), and has finely cut leaves and yellow, daisy-like flowers in summer. In many parts of Asia a variety of this chrysanthemum is grown for its edible leaves.

GROWING NOTES

These fast-growing and vigorous plants can be grown in most climates. Sow seed *in situ* in the fall or spring in warmer locations, or indoors in early spring in colder climates. Grow them in sun in light, moderately fertile, well-drained soil. *C. carinatum* will benefit from some wind protection and likes slightly acid soil.

Opposite: The aptly named *C. carinatum* 'Court Jesters' are colorful and easy to grow.

Above: *C. coronarium* is a bushy annual species of Mediterranean origin.

COSMOS BIPINNATUS
MEXICAN ASTER

The older varieties of annual *Cosmos* tend to be tall and floppy, growing to 5 ft (1.5 m) high, but modern cultivars are more compact. Other things about *Cosmos* have changed too. The flowers of the early garden strains tended to come in tones of pinks, pale reds, lilac, purples, and white, but now strong yellow, orange, and clear red tones are also available. Long-lasting as cut flowers and suitable for cottage gardens, all have graceful, feathery foliage and large flowers over a long period from summer to frost. Tall growers are useful for back-of-the-border planting, lower ones as fillers. *C. sulphureus* is a more sprawling, coarser-foliaged plant with yellow, red, and orange flowers.

Opposite: *Cosmos* usually comes in many hues, such as pink, crimson, lilac, purple, and white.

Above: There are modern strains that include yellow and orange.

GROWING NOTES
Cosmos will grow almost anywhere but the tropics, and is easy to grow even in dry and infertile soils. Rich soil will result in lush growth at the expense of flowering. These plants need full sun and shelter from wind, and may need staking on a windy site. Dead-heading will prolong flowering, and plants may self-sow.

CROCUS SPECIES & HYBRIDS
CROCUS

First recorded in Crete in 1500 BC for its dyeing properties, the dried yellow-orange stigmas of saffron (*Crocus sativus*) have been a valuable source of trade for centuries. It is still one of the most expensive spices. Similar in appearance to their distant *Colchicum* relatives, crocus have three rather than six stamens. There's a wide choice of these goblet-shaped gems, with over 80 species and many hybrids available: choose from pure colors, stripes or two-tone—or lightly fragrant.

A few crocus, such as *C. kotschyanus* subsp. *kotschyanus* and *C. speciosus*, are fall-flowering. Peeping through the snow from late winter or early spring are the *C. chrysanthus* varieties, usually in cream and yellow, or with markings of bronze or purple; the species blooms in bright orange. *C. tommasinianus* is a beautiful, tall, dainty lavender species—sometimes with a white throat—with reddish purple hybrids. One of the most popular and striking groups comprises the *C. vernus* varieties known as Dutch crocus, usually flowering in blue, purple or white.

Raising their heads towards the sun, *Crocus serotinus* subsp. *salzmannii* look divine planted in a woodland garden.

Right: *C. tommasinianus.*

Opposite: The vertical silvery green stripe is a characteristic of the crocus leaf.

GROWING NOTES

Plant spring-flowering crocus in the fall or 3–4 weeks before the last frost, as most crocus need a cold snap for good growth; the most popular varieties (with a few exceptions) enjoy temperatures of between 5°F and –4°F (–15°C and –20°C). In milder climates, refrigerator chilling for several weeks will not guarantee success beyond the first year. Best grown in an alpine house are *C. hadriaticus* and *C. tournefortii*. Mass plant for stunning effect and leave to naturalize under deciduous trees or in lawns; the corms multiply readily from bulblets. Fully mature leaves often appear after the flowers have faded; mow lawns once the foliage has died back. Crocus are ideal bulbs for rock gardens, borders, containers, and short-term indoor display.

CYCLAMEN SPECIES & HYBRIDS
PERSIAN VIOLET

Above: *C. hederifolium*.

Opposite: Position florist's cyclamen in bright, indirect light with fresh air, and regularly place them outdoors at night so they escape the drying heat.

The coy-looking cyclamen display their elegant and delicate twisting petals face-down. Adding highlights to a dormant fall garden, their often fragrant blooms of pink, red, magenta, lavender, deep purple or crisp white emerge from the corm, which nestles at ground level. The heart-shaped foliage—decorated with variegated colorings, silvery green blotches, marbled patterns or toothed edges—makes cyclamen an attractive ground cover.

GROWING NOTES

Originally from the Mediterranean and southwest Asia, cyclamen need cool weather and well-drained soil to thrive. Two favorites are the hardy *C. hederifolium*, which flowers in late summer and early fall, and *C. coum*, which blooms in winter or early spring. Plant corms in early fall in drifts beneath deciduous trees or shrubs, and display the larger, scented varieties of florist's cyclamen (*C. persicum* and *C. persicum grandiflorum*) indoors or on a sheltered veranda. New varieties available have large, pendulous, two-tone flowers or ruffled petals.

DAHLIA SPECIES & CULTIVARS

DAHLIA

It may be the national flower of Mexico, but worldwide "dahliamania" affects thousands of gardeners who live and breathe "exhibition" dahlias, devoting their gardens to them, forming specialist societies and clubs aimed at advancing dahlia growing, and holding annual events to exhibit this exquisite range of blooms. Dahlias are divided into categories that vary between societies, but the classifications include descriptive names such as Anemone-flowered, Collarette, Waterlily, Decorative, Ball, Pompon, Cactus, Semicactus, Single, Stellar, Orchid, Peony, and Chrysanthemum. The sizes too are diverse, ranging from dwarfs and miniatures through to giants. Choose single colors, bicolors, blends, pastels, striped, and even variegated forms for summer and fall flowers. Generally grown from tubers, "exhibition" dahlias fall into a class of their own.

Opposite: The red dahlia flowers are subdued and contrast well with the deep maroon foliage.

Above: An exquisite pink Pompon variety.

Bedding dahlias, on the other hand, are smaller forms, growing to 24–30 in (60–75 cm), and although they form tubers when they are mature, they are usually grown from seed and treated as annuals. The fall-flowering tree or bell tree dahlias (*D. imperialis*), with their bamboo-like stems and lavender-pink flowers, can grow 8–33 ft (2.5–10 m) tall, depending on the climate. They can be purchased through specialist perennial growers; single and double white varieties are also available.

GROWING NOTES

Dahlias grow in most climates apart from tropical. They grow best in sunny, sheltered, well-drained positions. Taller or top-heavy varieties may require staking. Plant tubers during spring after last frosts, and keep them well watered during the summer months. At the end of the growing season, leave them in the ground; in frost-prone areas, dig up the tubers and store them through winter. Propagate from seed or cuttings; alternatively, divide tubers, keeping an "eye" attached to each. Prune tree dahlias after flowering by about a third, and to propagate them, divide tubers or layer pieces of cut stem in a trench, then cover with soil. Later remove and plant the new shoots.

Opposite: Grow pure white dahlia varieties on their own, or use them to offset a bold color.

Above: Dahlia blooms make bold displays, either in the garden or as cut flowers. Mass plant them for a dramatic effect.

DOROTHEANTHUS BELLIDIFORMIS
SYN. *MESEMBRYANTHEMUM CRINIFLORUM*
LIVINGSTONE DAISY

Livingstone daisies will put on a dazzling display in sunny gardens.

Although *Dorotheanthus* is still widely referred to simply as *Mesembryanthemum*, its current botanical name means "Dorothy's flower" and was bestowed by a German botanist in honor of his mother. The common name ice plant comes from the glistening surface cells on the succulent leaves that give plants the appearance of being coated with ice. No wonder Livingstone daisies command such attention when they flower en masse in winter in their native South Africa. The flowers close in dull light, so in gardens they are grown as a carpeting annual to flower in spring and summer—which they do in dazzling shades of yellow, pink, red, and white.

GROWING NOTES

These drought-hardy plants can be planted in the fall in warm climates, or in spring in cooler places when danger of frost has passed. They must be planted in full sun and kept on the dry side once established. Ice plants thrive in sandy, sharply drained soil in hot dry places, such as rock gardens, gaps in paving, and on banks; and being salt resistant, they excel as seaside planting.

ERYTHRONIUM SPECIES
DOG'S-TOOTH VIOLET

Nodding, lily-like flowers adorn these small, spring-flowering plants, often with marbled foliage. The petals may be reflexed, curling upwards in an array of colors, including white, yellow, rose, lavender, mauve, and plum. With around 20 species and many cultivars, there may be just one or several flowers to each stem. Plant heights reach a tidy 4–14 in (10–35 cm). The common name dog's-tooth violet refers to the canine-like appearance of the bulb. Widely cultivated are *E. dens-canis, E. americanum, E. californicum, E. revolutum,* and *E. tuolumnense.*

GROWING NOTES

Most species are native to the north-western United States and western Canada; *E. dens-canis* originated in Europe and Asia. Grow these plants in cool- and cold-climate gardens, providing humus-rich, well-drained soil in a partially shady location. *Erythronium* resents being disturbed, so plant *in situ* during fall, 3 in (8 cm) deep and 4 in (10 cm) apart. When the bulbs become crowded, propagate by division in the fall or after the flowers are spent. Some species produce new bulbs on stolons.

Dog's-tooth violet are perfect for tucking into shady pockets of rock gardens, or planting in drifts in the dappled light provided by deciduous trees in a woodland garden.

FREESIA SPECIES & HYBRIDS

FREESIA

The freesia's trademark is its distinctive, sweet fragrance, wafting through the air, detected long before the flower is seen. The wild scented species have yellow, pink or purple flowers; the stems of modern hybrids are laden with blooms in cream, white, yellow, pink, cerise, purple, red, and orange. Flowering during middle to late winter through to mid-spring, freesias are excellent cut flowers for bouquets and vases; for lasting freshness, they are best kept in a cool room. Choose scentless varieties if you find the fragrance overpowering.

Above: En masse, freesias create scented borders.

Opposite: With long stems and fragrant blooms, freesias can be picked for indoor display or bouquets.

GROWING NOTES

Native to southern and southwest South Africa, freesias are suited to zones with a warm to cool range, frost-free or near frost-free. Freesias can be grown in greenhouses all year round. Depending on the location, plant corms 1–2 in (3–5 cm) deep and 1 in (3 cm) apart from early to late fall; plant in spring for summer blooms in cooler areas. Choose a sunny position in moist but well-drained soil; water thoroughly during the growing season only. In some areas it's considered a weed, as the corms multiply readily.

FRITILLARIA SPECIES
FRITILLARY

Related to the iris and tulip, these interesting bulbs are a delightful addition to spring-flowering rock, alpine or woodland gardens. Aptly named, the snake's head lily (*F. meleagris*)—with its chequered patterns of green, purple, magenta or white—is simply exquisite. The majestic crown imperial (*F. imperialis*) is a striking lily with red, orange or yellow bell-shaped flowers topped by a whorl of spiky narrow leaves. Other species include the dainty olive green *F. acmopetala*, and *F. pallidiflora*, with soft yellow flowers veined lime green or burgundy. For impact, plant the deep purple *F. persica*, which grows to 3–4 ft (90 cm–1.2 m).

The fascinating snake's head lily (*F. meleagris*).

GROWING NOTES

In cool, cold and frost-prone climates, plant bulbs in late summer or early fall. Prepare the bed in full sun, or light shade in warmer regions, incorporating organic matter into well-drained soil. Plant *F. imperialis* and *F. persica* at least 8 in (20 cm) deep and spaced 1 ft (30 cm) apart; plant all other species 3 in (8 cm) deep and 6 in (15 cm) apart. Plant in clumps and divide when overcrowded. Fritillary can be grown as container plants.

GLADIOLUS SPECIES & HYBRIDS
GLADIOLI

Above: Look for species with delicate patterns if others are too bold for your garden. Gladioli are also known as sword lily.

Opposite: *G. communis* subsp. *byzantinus* (planted here with *Ixia viridiflora* in the background) are suitable for colder areas, grow up to 3 ft (1 m), and don't need to be dug up each year.

Not all gladioli are as exuberant as those embraced by Dame Edna Everage, the entertainer! This large group of multicolored plants has hundreds of species and hybrids in a variety of shapes and sizes, suitable for a variety of tastes—from the delicately subtle, spring-flowering species *G. carneus* or *G.* x *colvilei* to the night-fragrant *G. tristis*, blooming in late winter or early spring. But the best known are the large-flowered summer-flowering cultivars, widely grown for cut flower displays and exhibitions. Reaching 3–5 ft (1–1.5 m), with frilled, ruffled, semiruffled or plain petals, gladioli come in solid colors or combinations that include red, salmon, pink, yellow, orange, violet, green, white, and pastels. Other hybrid groups include the Primulinus (miniature) and Nanus (butterfly) varieties. The early-flowering, hardy gladioli (*G. communis* subsp. *byzantinus*), with their magenta-colored petals, are suitable for colder areas and don't need to be dug up annually.

GROWING NOTES

Most gladioli originate in South African- or Mediterranean-type climates. Plant invasive types in pots. Grow in a sunny, wind-protected position, in sandy or loamy, well-drained soil. Plant the corms, pointy end up, 4 in (10 cm) deep and around 7 in (17 cm) apart. Start planting large-flowering hybrids in early spring and plant successively for continuous summer flowers; hardy species can be planted in the fall along with spring-flowering varieties in frost-free areas. In cold climates, overwinter early-flowering types in a cool greenhouse. Provide ample, deep waterings during the growing period. Tall varieties may need staking. Cut flower spikes early in the morning when the first florets are opening, and leave two to four leaves to aid maturing corms. After flowering, dig the corms up when the foliage starts to die off, leave to dry for several weeks, then remove and store corms and cormels.

Above: Plant small species gladioli en masse along borders where they can be seen and enjoyed.

Opposite: For a dramatic color combination, plant large-flowered hybrids in vibrant red and rich mauve next to each other.

HEMEROCALLIS HYBRIDS
DAYLILIES

Each bloom may live for only one day, but what a spectacular day! Single plants may produce 15–40 buds on each scape, providing flowers over a long period during summer; the common name of daylily aptly describes the longevity of each bloom. Derived from two Greek words, its botanic name *Hemerocallis* means "beauty" and "day," although a few species and hybrids are fragrant, nocturnal bloomers. Choose single colors, blends or bicolors, flecked or speckled petals or colored throats. Shapes include star, ruffled, trumpet, and double; sizes and heights range from miniature to large, with thousands of named cultivars available; and some are scented.

Hybridization techniques produce these stunning plants in every rainbow color except blue—from yellow, melon, rose, red, mahogany, and purple in pastel and bright shades.

GROWING NOTES

Drought resistant and suitable for cool temperate to subtropical climates, daylilies can bloom from early spring until fall frost. Plant in sun or part shade en masse, or in containers. Select from evergreen, dormant or semi-evergreen varieties. Divide *Hemerocallis* every three years in the fall or spring.

HIPPEASTRUM HYBRIDA VARIETIES
AMARYLLIS

Looking for a showstopper? Try the big, bold blooms of hippeastrum hybrids. These grow in shades of red, maroon, orange, pink or white (yellow forms are rare) as single or bicolors. The flowers may be streaked, veined or edged as doubles, semidoubles and miniatures, flowering from midspring to early summer in gardens, or "forced" to bloom indoors during winter in cooler climates. Bloom numbers vary from two to eight, depending on the cultivar. Originating in South America, *Hippeastrum* species bloom in similar colors but with more intricate, delicate shapes.

GROWING NOTES

These plants are suited to frost-free, warm gardens, but in colder areas grow them indoors or in a greenhouse. Plant hippeastrum hybrids while they are dormant, during the fall or early spring, in a sunny, protected position, with the bulb neck above soil level. Plant the bulbs 10 in (25 cm) apart, or with a quarter of the bulb above potting mix level in a pot. Remove and plant individual bulblets from mature bulbs, or store them for the next season. Alternatively, transplant the whole bulb into a larger pot. Keep bulbs dry after flowering.

Above: Also known as Dutch hybrids, hippeastrum are striking garden plants in a warm location.

Opposite: Forced flowering allows festive red blooms like this one to be enjoyed indoors in northern hemisphere winters.

HYACINTHUS ORIENTALIS HYBRIDS

HYACINTH

According to Greek mythology, Hyacinthus was a young Spartan who was accidentally killed by a discus, either thrown by Apollo or blown off course by the wind god, Zephrus. Hyacinthus's blood was turned into a flower by Apollo, and now each spring his memory is revived.

Popularized during the Victorian era, the waxy-looking, elegant *H. orientalis* has been hybridized in Holland for decades, and many named cultivars are available, known as 'Dutch hybrids'. The intoxicatingly fragrant, star-shaped single or double florets bloom in pure white, cream, pastel pink or blue, salmon, and apricot through to the richer colors of deep blue, purple, red, hot pink, and bright yellow. Plants grow to around 1 ft (30 cm) in height. Hyacinths are popular as indoor flowering plants for spring or increasingly, as a Christmas display in the United Kingdom and the United States. Bedding hyacinths labelled as 'Giant' can be bought, although generally, smaller varieties are best planted en masse. Less common and less flamboyant are the 'Roman hybrids' (of *H. o.* var. *albulus*).

An ancient Persian proverb advises, "If you have two coins, use one to buy bread, the other to buy hyacinths, for the joy of your spirit."

GROWING NOTES

In the garden, hyacinths can be left to naturalize, producing many small bulblets that will flower in subsequent years. Plant or divide during late summer or fall in organic-rich, well-drained soil in a sunny or lightly shaded position. Space bulbs approximately 6 in (15 cm) deep and apart, but adjust these distances for larger bulbs, which can be up to 6–7 in (16–19 cm) in circumference. Those grown for indoor displays are best replaced annually, as after the first year, blooms can be disappointing. For more information on growing hyacinths indoors, see "Forcing bulbs for indoor display" (page 471).

Plant single colors in groups of odd numbers, such as three's, or for a better visual effect, use two contrasting colors together. Indoors, display these scented blooms in a decorative bowl.

IMPATIENS BALSAMINA & I. WALLERIANA

BUSY LIZZIE

Above: Single- and double-flowered impatiens, also known as balsam, come in a huge range of colors.

Opposite: If you prefer subtle flowers, then New Guinea hybrids may not be for you, but they do make vivacious pot plants and suit tropical gardens.

Impatiens have undergone a transformation in recent years, and are now more varied and sophisticated. But they are still among the easiest plants to grow, bringing color to a semishaded area. Both the familiar single and the rose-like double flowers of the newer types come in almost every color imaginable, except yellow and blue. Mixed planting creates vibrant color, while blocks of one color produce a more restful effect. Most garden impatiens are derived from the African perennial species *I. walleriana* and the bushy annual *I. balsamina*, which hails from parts of Asia. As they are frost tender, impatiens are commonly treated as annuals, although they will overwinter in warmer climates. The New Guinea hybrids have larger, often colorfully variegated leaves and broad-petaled flowers.

The botanical name *Impatiens* refers to busy Lizzie's impatience to reproduce itself by scattering seeds far and wide, for its seed capsules explode at the slightest touch. These adaptable plants can be used for massed displays or as clumps in the garden, and in containers and hanging baskets.

GROWING NOTES

Impatiens can be planted and will flower all year round in warm conditions, peaking in spring to fall. They are popular house or conservatory plants in cool climates. They grow and flower best in moist, partly shady areas, although the New Guinea hybrids won't flower well in heavy shade. All will adapt to almost full sun if given a cool root run and protection from direct sun in midsummer and in hotter climates. Give indoor plants bright, filtered light and water them sparingly in winter. Regular trimming prevents them from becoming leggy and encourages new blooms.

Above: Impatiens can be grown in dappled shade in the garden.

Opposite: They also excel as potted plants.

IRIS SPECIES & HYBRIDS
IRIS

Iris are named after the Greek rainbow goddess: with today's vast range of multicolored cultivars, it's a fitting label. Often grouped together, Bearded iris, Flag iris, and Water iris grow from rhizomatous roots and are actually not true bulbs. The true bulbs fall within three groups. There are the Reticulatas—these fragrant dwarf species and hybrids are also known as "net iris," reflecting the bulbs' loose, fibrous skin. Mainly blooming in purple-blue colors with white, yellow or orange markings, the most common is *I. reticulata* and its derivatives.

Lesser known are Juno iris, with their sweetcorn-like leaves. The easy-care Xiphium Group includes the Spanish iris (*I. xiphium*), the so-called English iris (*I. xiphioides* syn. *I. latifolia*) and, frequently used by florists, the popular Dutch iris (*I. xiphium* x *I. tingitana*) cultivars.

Opposite: *Iris reticulata.*

Above: Dutch iris hybrid.

Following pages: A purple-flowered Dutch iris.

GROWING NOTES
Cultivation requirements vary between the groups, but generally these irises are best suited to climates with hot, dry summers and mild winters. As iris originated in alkaline soils, an application of lime or dolomite is often recommended, depending on the soil type.

LATHYRUS ODORATUS
SWEET PEA

One of the few climbing annuals, sweet peas have fascinated British horticulturists since they were introduced from Sicily in the 17th century. The oldest cultivars have smaller flowers and a sweeter scent than modern cultivars. The wavy-petaled 'Spencer' types, developed in the early 20th century, laid the foundation for modern breeding efforts, which have given us larger flowers, non-climbing varieties, more heat-tolerant plants and flowers in almost every color, including bicolors, picotees, and blooms with ripples and speckles. Only yellow eludes the breeders, who are also trying to give us back the old-fashioned sweet pea fragrance we yearn for.

Sweet peas come in both pastel and vibrant shades, and include almost every color but yellow.

GROWING NOTES
Sweet peas do best in cool climates and will grow in warm temperate zones, but they are not suitable for the tropics. Sow seed indoors or *in situ* in the fall or spring depending on the climate, to flower in winter, spring or summer, according to the climate and cultivar. They need full sun, and limey, enriched, moist but well-drained soil, protection from wind, and support for their climbing habit.

LILIUM SPECIES & HYBRIDS

LILY

The exotic-sounding Turk's-cap, the heavily-spotted tiger lily (*L. lancifolium*) and the white-petaled madonna lily (*L. candidum*)—these are just a few descriptive names owned by different liliums. Such a diverse range of plants can't be covered within a few pages: not only are there around 100 species of lilies, but also hybridizing has led to a mouth-watering array of colors (all except blue), with about 7000 registered varieties! Flower shapes fall into various classifications, including Trumpet- or Bowl-shaped, Recurved (Turk's-cap) or Flat, borne in late spring and summer; heights range from dwarf to tall, back-of-the-border varieties. For colorful and fragrant blooms, cut flowers, container plants, or pure eye-candy, look no further.

Popular hybrids include the early blooming Asiatics, often sold as cut flowers or pot plants; the mid- to late-season Trumpet varieties, including those derived from *L. regale*; and the spectacular Orientals, with heavy perfumes, that flower late-season. Flowering midseason are the spotted Martagon hybrids, derived from *L. martagon* and *L. hansonii*. Borne on tall stems and mostly Turk's-cap-shaped are the American hybrids that include the Bellingham hybrids. In the northern

Opposite: The American Turk's-cap lily, *Lilium superbum*, with its striking orange to red maroon-spotted petals.

Above: *Lilium longiflorum* is called the Easter lily and is often "forced" to bloom early in the northern hemisphere; in the southern hemisphere, gardeners know it as the November lily.

Opposite: With pink petals edged in white and with dark speckles, the Oriental *Lilium* 'Stargazer' is a popular, fragrant choice as a cut flower.

hemisphere, the pure white *L. longiflorum* is called the Easter lily and is often "forced" to bloom early; southern hemisphere gardeners know it as the November lily.

GROWING NOTES

Liliums are best suited to cold, cool, and frost-free gardens. Generally, lilies prefer well-drained, organic-rich, acidic soils, but some, particularly modern hybrids, tolerate lime. Protect liliums from strong winds, and ideally locate them in semishade or dappled light, although full sun may be suitable for some varieties. Select appropriate species and cultivars for your location, and check their cultural requirements and propagation methods that vary, depending on whether it's by division or from bulblets, bulbils, and scales. There are many specialist growers, suppliers, societies, and clubs that can offer advice and choice.

MATTHIOLA INCANA
STOCK

There are tall and low forms of stock or gillyflower, single- and double-flowered forms, and both pastel and strong shades.

Cultivated forms of M. *incana* are grown in gardens and for the cut-flower trade as an annual, but may overwinter in mild areas. The clove-scented flowers come in diverse colors that include pastel and strong shades, from apple blossom pink, through rose, lavender, and purple shades to magenta, deep mulberry plus creams and white. It is easier to mix a planting of these colors than to try to make a statement with one. Although there are single- and double-flowered forms, the best strains have a predominance of double flowers. There are tall and dwarf growers, the flower spikes borne above clusters of gray-green foliage. M. *longipetala* subsp. *bicornis* is the night-scented stock.

GROWING NOTES

Stock will grow in all climates but the tropics, and it needs full sun and wind protection. Stake the taller types. Grow stock in moderately fertile, well-drained, neutral to slightly alkaline soil. Sow or plant *in situ* in the fall in warm areas, spring in cool zones, or in seed trays.

NEMESIA SPECIES & CULTIVARS

NEMESIA

Compact, bushy, and low-growing, the annual *Nemesia strumosa* becomes smothered by two-lipped flowers in dazzling blends of reds, pinks, oranges, yellows, purple, and white. When planted closely, they provide festive color from late winter through spring. Since *Nemesia* thrive in drier conditions, they are a good choice for rock gardens and will brighten containers of any kind. They have become more fashionable in recent years, with different colored cultivars and more perennial species grown as annuals, extending the color range to include blues, pastels, and striking bicolors.

Vibrant *Nemesia* will brighten up the garden in late winter.

GROWING NOTES

Nemesia grow in most cool to warm climates, but they don't tolerate tropical heat and humidity. In warm zones, sow or plant them in the fall, but in cool climates delay planting until spring. They do best in full sun and moderately fertile soil with good drainage. Pinch out the growing tips when the plants are small to encourage bushiness and greater flowering. The flowering period is short but you can encourage them to flower from the lower stems if you cut them back when the rate of flowering slows.

OXALIS SPECIES
SORREL

Largely native to South Africa and South America, this unfortunate genus of more than 800 species has been the target of many gardeners' curses, as the rampant weed varieties (sourgrass, soursob or wood sorrel) spread by seed and underground bulbils. However, don't overlook the useful slow-growing ornamental species and hybrids without the "runaway" characteristics. Many oxalis have clover-like leaves, while others are finely pinnate or have intriguing triangular-shaped foliage. Explore the summer deciduous options, including the many colorful hybrid forms of the winter-flowering *O. hirta*. The frost-hardy *O. massoniana* has orange-toned flowers and the popular *O. adenophylla* has lilac-pink veined petals and fine greenish gray leaves. Selected forms have purple foliage.

Above: Ornamental varieties of oxalis are suitable as colorful groundcovers or trailing container specimens.

Opposite: *Oxalis purpurea* 'Alba' has funnel-shaped, satiny white flowers.

GROWING NOTES

Plant winter-hardy species in the fall and those susceptible to frost in spring or summer. Locate in full sun to partial shade, in well-drained soil or potting mix, and keep moist during the growth period. Grow in containers, hanging baskets, rock gardens, alpine- or greenhouses. Buy oxalis from specialist nurseries and seek advice on suitable varieties.

PAPAVER SPECIES
POPPY

Few sights gladden a gardener's heart more than a field of poppies. Although perennial, *P. nudicaule*, the Iceland poppy, is usually grown as an annual. Yellow, orange, pink, and cream are the predominant tones of the crinkly, crepey, cup-shaped flowers, but modern breeding is giving us strains of both richer and pastel colors with ever-larger flowers and stronger, sometimes shorter, stems. They bloom in late winter and early spring in warmer areas, in summer in cooler climates, and they make excellent cut flowers. *P. lacinatum* produces huge, fully double, deeply frilled and feathery flowers atop 3 ft (1 m) stems.

The wild form of *P. rhoeas* has delicate, brilliant scarlet flowers, usually with a black blob at the base of the petals, and is known as the corn or field poppy or the Flanders or Gallipoli poppy, for it is the symbol of fallen World War I soldiers. *P. commutatum* is a close relative and is sometimes confused with this species; both excel in meadow or wild gardens.

The original cultivated form of *P. rhoeas* was raised in the 1880s by the vicar of Shirley in England from one white-edged flower among a patch of scarlet field poppies. Today we have single and double-flowered strains of Shirley poppy in shades

Opposite: Poppies are colorful and among the easiest plants to grow.

Above: The Shirley poppy.

of rich pink through salmon to white, plus bicolors, speckles, and picotees. A favorite in cottage gardens, they are a delight when massed or used as accent plants, or mixed with perennials.

GROWING NOTES

Annual poppies are among the easiest flowers to grow in most climates, provided they are planted in sun and well-drained soil. Sow or plant them in late summer or fall, or in early spring in cooler areas. Avoid overwatering as the crowns will rot. Liquid feed growing plants.

Opposite: The Shirley poppy, derived from *P. rhoeas*, has single- and double-flowered forms.

Above: The corn or field poppy, *P. rhoeas*, will self-seed with abandon in wild or meadow gardens.

Above: Red and pink are popular colors for geraniums, but they come in a host of other shades.

Opposite: Ivy-leaved geraniums spill from window boxes and hanging baskets in many European countries in summer.

PELARGONIUM SPECIES
GERANIUM

Red zonal geraniums in terracotta pots or the ivy-leaved types cascading from balcony window boxes are synonymous with European summers. Arguably the world's most commonly grown flowering pot plants, yet rarely acknowledged by their correct botanical name, "geraniums" are not members of the geranium family (Geraniaceae), but in fact belong to the genus *Pelargonium*. The zonal types, *P.* x *hortorum*, get their name from their horseshoe-shaped leaf marking, and the ivy-leaved varieties, *P. peltatum* hybrids, from their foliage shape.

Pelargoniums must be the plant most commonly grown by non-gardeners, even if they have only a single potted plant on a windowsill. The zonals are also widely admired as colorful bedding plants in public parks, and the trailing ivy-leaved hybrids are increasingly grown as landscape plants. After centuries of hybridization, zonal *Pelargonium* flowers come in almost every color but yellow and blue, while the ivy-leaved types are usually red, pink or white. Both types will flower continuously for long periods in warm conditions and will overwinter in warm climates, but being frost-tender they are commonly grown as annuals.

Right: Commonly grown in pots, in warm climates *Pelargonium* can also be grown in gardens.

Opposite: There are hundreds of varieties of zonal pelargoniums.

GROWING NOTES

Pelargoniums are so widely grown that you would be forgiven for believing that they are easy-care plants. While some are, others are so difficult to either grow or propagate that they remain collector's items. Traditionally propagated from cuttings, some newer strains come true from seed. The latest breeding technology has produced pollen-free zonals that go on flowering for a long season without producing the unsightly seed heads that mar the appearance of some plants. Their main growing requirements are good light and well-drained soil or potting media. Geraniums are prone to fungal disease, and require regular watering, feeding, and pruning. Ivy-leaved geraniums cope with humidity better and are less troubled by rust and whitefly.

PENSTEMON HYBRIDS
BEARD TONGUE

Tall spikes of tubular *Penstemon* flowers are graceful additions to the late summer garden. Although there are many subshrubs and perennials in the genus, some of the showiest garden hybrids that can't be guaranteed to make it through a cold winter will flower reliably in their first year to grow as annuals. Tall varieties up to 2 ft (80 cm) are excellent as cutting or border plants, while *P. barbatus* 'Cambridge' mix— flowering in shades of rose, pink, blue, and purple, with gray-green foliage—has a neater habit, growing to 1 ft (30 cm), making it a smart choice for containers and bedding.

Some strains of *Penstemon* are marginally frost hardy and best grown as annuals in cold areas.

GROWING NOTES

Although many perennial *Penstemon* may take up to six months to flower from seed, the strains grown as annuals will flower as early as 16–20 weeks from sowing. As they may be marginally frost hardy, sowing and planting times should be programmed to avoid frost danger. Grow them in full sun and well-drained soil where they are sheltered from wind. In the right microclimate they may even overwinter.

PERICALLIS X HYBRIDA SYN. SENECIO X HYBRIDUS
CINERARIA

Few mass displays command as much attention as a gathering of cinerarias. In late winter and early spring, the brightly colored pink, carmine, purple, mauve, and white clusters of daisy-like flowers create drama in a shady spot. But they will only do this in a garden setting in temperate areas, for they are both frost tender and intolerant of tropical humidity and heavy rain. In the right location, cineraria are a bushy perennial, but mostly they're grown as an annual, and in cold climates you usually see them potted as conservatory or shadehouse plants. They are a popular florist line for indoor decoration in winter.

A mass display of cinerarias is an arresting sight.

GROWING NOTES

Both tall and compact dwarf types can be grown in borders for a mass display. Plant them in cool positions in filtered sunlight in moist, organically-enriched but well-drained soil, or in pots protected from frost and heat. Sow seed into trays in late summer to fall and gradually increase the pot size. Liquid feed plants regularly once they start budding and flowering, and protect them from aphids, leaf miner, and powdery mildew.

PETUNIA X HYBRIDA

PETUNIA

Grandiflora petunias have the largest flowers, which are generally fluted or ruffled. They need careful watering, for they will collapse with heavy overhead watering.

The most popular of all summer annuals and one of the most colorful, after centuries of breeding and improvement petunias now come in hues of every color except orange. There are straight colors, bicolors, throated flowers, and veined and picoteed blooms, which may be single, double or frilled. Flower size varies too, from the 'Grandiflora' types that have, as the name implies, the largest, showiest flowers on rather sprawling plants, down to the 'Millifloras', which produce masses of miniature flowers on extremely compact bushes. Categories of petunia are actually seed suppliers' classifications rather than strictly botanical ones; this is only one of a number of factors to consider when you are faced with the plethora of choice.

In recent years a new category—spreading petunias, which trail or cascade for over 3 ft (1 m)—has captured a lion's share of the international and competitive petunia market. Other qualities to consider are weather and disease tolerance, as well as the ability of plants to keep their shape after wind and rain. With so many petunias available there must be a petunia to suit every situation, from mass bedding and garden borders to hanging baskets, and tubs and troughs of all sizes.

GROWING NOTES

Sun-loving petunias will grow in almost all climates. The very fine seeds are best sown indoors, or plants can be purchased in spring or summer to flower in summer and fall.

Protect petunias from snails, and pinch out the growing tips when plants are 3–4 in (8–10 cm) high to encourage bushy growth. Water regularly to establish, then only water when the soil dries out, as overwatering, especially overhead watering, will encourage fungal disease. Overfertilizing will result in an abundance of foliage rather than flowers. After the first flush of flowers, cut the plants back to encourage a second blooming.

Opposite: Petunias can be bought as straight colors or in many blends.

Above: Use white petunias to tone down more vibrant planting schemes.

POLYANTHUS

Polyanthus primroses, like their relatives *Primula malacoides* we have considered elsewhere (see "Pastel," page 428), are perennial plants in cool climates, but are often treated as annuals in gardens where summers are dry, or grown for short-term potted color. Enthusiasts started hybridizing the English primrose (*Primula vulgaris*) with other European primroses back in the 17th century. Modern polyanthus share the early flowering characteristics of these ancestors, so are highly valued for their winter and early spring blooms, but the enormous color range available today would amaze those early breeders. Multicolored displays look good in nurseries and help sell these charmers, although plantings of single or sympathetic colors generally work better than contrasting colors.

From late winter, brighten up gardens and patio pots with the vivid colors of polyanthus. Display them indoors too.

GROWING NOTES

Polyanthus prefer light shade in most areas but will tolerate full sun in cool zones. They can be displayed indoors for a short time. The soil should be enriched before planting and always kept just moist but well-drained. Regular liquid feeds and removal of spent flower stems will encourage new blooms, while snails and slugs must be kept at bay.

RANUNCULUS ASIATICUS
PERSIAN BUTTERCUP

With their ruffles of tissue-like petals, these vibrant plants bring cheer to late winter, spring, or even summer gardens, depending on the location. Ranunculi colors extend from the warm tones of orange, yellow, and reds to dark purple, almost black, as well as pastel pinks, cream, and white—but not blues. Persian buttercup is often sold as semidouble or double types, with petal formations like camellias or small peonies, as in the 'Bloomingdale' hybrid range. Heights reach 15 in (38 cm), with dwarf forms at 8–10 in (20–25 cm). Available as multicolored and single varieties, ranunculi are ideal as cut flowers. Plant them en masse for a stunning display.

GROWING NOTES

Plant ranunculi in early to mid fall in warm and cool areas; in cold, frost-free climates it may be preferable to plant in spring for late spring and summer flowering. Ensure the "claws" of the tubers point downwards. Plant them 1–2 in (3–5 cm) deep and 6 in (15 cm) apart in moist, well-drained soil, and water well during the growing and flowering seasons. Ranunculi are best treated as annuals with fresh tubers planted each year.

Opposite: Colorful ranunculi are often planted with anemones, which bloom at the same time and look similar.

Above: Double-flowered varieties are reminiscent of small peonies.

SALPIGLOSSIS SINUATA
PAINTED TONGUE

Salpiglossis come in a wide range of colors.

These upright half-hardy annuals or short-lived perennials are related to petunias but grow much taller, to 2 ft (60 cm). Their heavily veined, gold-streaked, trumpet-shaped flowers come in an array of rich colors that include yellows and oranges, deep reds and pinks, bluish purple, and some unusual dark velvety shades. They are trickier to grow than most annuals and hence relatively uncommon, but there are rewards if you do succeed. These multipurpose flowers can be grown for cutting and for background in borders, as well as in greenhouses, conservatories, and for potted color.

GROWING NOTES

Painted tongue likes conditions to be neither too hot nor too cold. Keep seed in the dark until it has germinated. The key to success is to plant acclimatized seedlings immediately after the last spring frost but well before the heat of summer. They must have excellent drainage, or they will rot, and a sunny aspect sheltered from wind. Pinch out the growing points of small plants to encourage bushiness, and water and fertilize only moderately. The plants may need staking.

SCHIZANTHUS PINNATUS, SCHIZANTHUS X WISETONENSIS

POOR MAN'S ORCHID

Like *Salpiglossis*, these plants originated in Chile and are related to the petunia. In spring and summer they put on a generous and colorful display of their beautiful, orchid-like tubular, two-lipped flowers that come in shades of pink, purple, mauve, red, white or yellow, all with contrasting gold-speckled throats. One species is *S. pinnatus*, an upright bushy annual with pale green fern-like foliage; garden hybrids and strains are derived from it and from *S. x wisetonensis*.

GROWING NOTES

Liking neither excessive heat nor cold, *Schizanthus* can be grown for massed garden displays in temperate climates but, even so, they do best grown in pots that can be brought inside once they are in flower. In colder climates they must be grown indoors or in a conservatory. Sow seed in late summer to winter or in spring in cold areas, and pinch out the growing tips of young plants to encourage bushy growth. Keep the soil or potting medium moist. Plants outdoors will do best in dappled shade or cool sun, and need shelter from wind.

Schizanthus can be grown in the garden but they are most commonly grown in pots for indoor display when in flower.

SOLENOSTEMON SCUTELLARIOIDES
SYN. *COLEUS* X *HYBRIDUS*
COLEUS

Coleus is grown for its striking foliage with colorful markings.

Native to southeast Asia, these evergreen, shrubby plants have a number of other botanical synonyms, but are usually referred to simply as *Coleus*. Unlike most annuals, they are grown for their multicolored foliage. Their serrated-edged oval leaves—patterned in splashes of green, red, purple, pink, burgundy, and yellow—are ideal for tropical gardens, or for creating the tropical or Balinese look in more temperate locations. They look striking as a background planting in garden borders, where plants will grow up to 2 ft (60 cm).

GROWING NOTES

In warm climates *Coleus* will grow as a perennial, but in more temperate locations it looks best grown as an annual, and since it will not tolerate low temperatures, it is usually grown as a house plant in cold climates. It can be propagated from seed or cuttings and should be planted in fertile soil in part shade, although it will tolerate full sun if given plenty of water. It is a thirsty plant, and if denied a drink, the leaves will be small and the growth stunted.

TORENIA FOURNIERI
WISHBONE FLOWER

Pert and pretty annuals and perennials, these compact, low-growing plants are delightful for pots and rock gardens, and as edging and fillers. This species is one of the few annuals that will grow in sun or shade. It loves tropical heat, humidity, and rainfall but will grow in cooler climates if it is planted in a sunny, warm spot, or in a conservatory or greenhouse in cold climates. The snapdragon-like, tubular two-lipped flowers of the original species are purplish blue with a yellow throat, but garden varieties, which flower in summer and fall, also come in pink and white, cool colors that are welcome in summer.

The original annual *Torenia* species is purplish blue, but garden varieties also come in shades of pink and white.

GROWING NOTES
Sow the very small seed in trays in spring and plant out when the weather warms up, definitely after the last frost in cold areas. Fertile, well-drained soil, with liberal additions of organic matter, will suit it best, and plants should be watered liberally, especially in hot, dry weather. Pinch growing shoots to promote branching and provide regular liquid feeds to encourage flowering.

TRILLIUM SPECIES & HYBRIDS
WAKE ROBIN

Also known as birthroot, these unusual and striking plants are ideal for woodland-style gardens.

With its display of three petals and three leaves, sepals and stamens, this hardy bulb makes an unusual spring or early summer show. Depending on the species, the colors may be white, yellow, green, pink or purple, and the flowers fragrant, stemless or miniature. Hardy, popular, and easy to grow is *T. grandiflorum*; its white flowers age to pink and are held above the deeply veined foliage. 'Flore Pleno' is a double form, 'Roseum' a pink variety. *Pseudotrillium rivale* (syn. *T. rivale*) has speckles and heart-shaped leaves.

GROWING NOTES

Found mainly in northern America and eastern Asia, most species prefer cold or cool, frost-prone climates with moist summers, but they will tolerate near frost-free areas. These plants require a shady, woodland setting, with dappled sun at most. Provide a moist soil, enriched with organic matter, and never allow it to completely dry out. Plant the rhizomes 3 in (8 cm) deep, allowing 1 ft (30 cm) between each. Leave them undisturbed. If multiplying by division in late summer or fall, replant them immediately. Trilliums can be grown in containers.

TULIPA CULTIVARS
tulip

With a satiny sheen to their petals, tulips bask in sunlight, showing off their rich tones. Planted in swathes like rivers, massed displays of single colors intoxicate. Blooms subtly streaked with a harmonious blend of colors entice, and those with fringed petals enchant.

With billions of colourful tulips grown commercially each year and over 3000 cultivated named varieties, it's no wonder they're divided into groups that often reflect their shape, color or blooming period—such as the Single Early and Double Early tulips. Named after the Dutch painter, Rembrandt tulips are imitations of those that commanded vast sums of money during the "Tulipmania" period in Holland between 1593 and 1637. Their unusual markings were actually caused by a virus, and modern varieties bear the same visual characteristics—but without the virus! Known also as Peony hybrids, the Double Late Group tulips are large and multipetaled; some are fragrant. Single-flowered Triumph hybrid buds are conical, opening as round; Darwin hybrids have very large blooms of various shapes, usually rounded. Hybrids of the Single Late Group bear large square or oval flowers on tall stems; and Lily-flowered hybrids are elegant with long, pointed, reflexed petals. Fringed varieties are just that: Parrot hybrids have deeply frilled, large and wavy petals, while hybrids of the late-flowering Viridiflora Group have fascinating, partially green petals.

Clockwise, from top left: Yellow and rich red stripes suit warm-colored garden schemes; the red Parrot tulips add visual interest; crimson-pink tulips with dark violet-blue hyacinths; and exquisite Lily-flowered hybrids with a backdrop of maroon-colored maple leaves.

Following pages: Pastel-colored tulips combined with warm tones.

Suitable for rock gardens or naturalizing in drifts are many of the Botanical tulips—species tulips or hybrids that have retained some original characteristics. These exquisite flowers look very different to the modern tulip and shouldn't be overlooked. The low-growing Kaufmanniana hybrids are similar to waterlilies, with very wide, bright petals; Fosteriana tulips are commonly called Emperor tulips. The foliage of the short, large-bloomed Greigii hybrids are often streaked with purple or brown.

Opposite, clockwise from top left: The faintly scented species *T. saxatalis* from Crete tilt their faces towards the sun; incorporate pink-red tulips with petals like flames in warm-colored designs; stunning two-toned tulips are also suitable for warm color schemes; and soft green and pale pink Parrot tulips show off their ruffled petals.

Left: Fresh red tulips planted en masse.

Above: Plant single-colored tulips on their own, or en masse with a sympathetic color.

Opposite: A tulip of the Rembrandt Group, often featured in old Dutch paintings. It has feathered white petals flushed with cardinal red.

GROWING NOTES

Tulip cultivars generally flower in early, mid- or late spring (some start in late winter). Grow them in cold, cool and near frost-free locations, although they are best in frost-prone areas. In warmer zones, refrigerator chilling may be successful in the first year only. Depending on the cultivar, climate, and location, plant bulbs in late fall or early winter. Plant them in full sun and well-drained soil so that the base of large bulbs are 6–8 in (15–20 cm) deep, and small bulbs are 4–5 in (10–12 cm) deep and 4–8 in (10–20 cm) apart. Lift most garden tulips (not rock garden varieties) after the foliage has died back; store in a dry, frost-free place until the following fall. Tulip cultivars make excellent garden container plants; use them for short-term indoor display.

VERBENA X HYBRIDA

VERBENA

Now here is an example of a plant undergoing a makeover. Recent hybrids that can be grown from cuttings or raised from seed to flower in their first year have transformed verbenas into more attractive and useful plants. There are upright, bushy forms for garden displays, and trailing types with long flowering periods that excel in hanging baskets and containers. Their sometimes fragrant flower clusters come in hot red, pink, and purple, and softer lavender, pink, white, and cream, and more recently, lovely shades of apricot and peach, some with interesting tonal variations within the clusters.

The two-toned flower clusters of modern verbenas look lovely in pots and baskets.

GROWING NOTES

Verbenas will grow well in most climates but they must have full sun and well-drained soil. Pinch out young plants to encourage bushiness, and trim after flowering to keep plants compact and to encourage new blooms. In warm climates they may overwinter and be brought back into growth if cut back in spring and fed. Avoid overpampering verbenas: they do not need very fertile soil or a lot of water, for these plants are susceptible to powdery mildew.

VIOLA

Above: A pretty cultivar in citrus colors called 'Oranges and Lemons'.

Opposite: *V. tricolor* has many charming common names and is the ancestor of hundreds of modern viola and pansy hybrids.

Once there was a clear distinction between pansies, which had faces, and violas, which didn't, but that's no longer true. The main difference in modern forms is that viola plants and flowers are generally smaller. The ancestor of most of today's garden varieties is the wild purple, yellow, and white *Viola tricolor*, native to most of Europe and Asia. It grows almost anywhere and self-seeds freely, giving rise to one of its common names, Johnny-jump-up. It is an ancient medicinal plant, and its juice was used in Oberon's love potion in Shakespeare's *A Midsummer Night's Dream*. This association with love has resulted in some other evocative names—heartsease, love-in-idleness, and love-lies-bleeding.

From *V. tricolor*, *V. cornuta*, and other voila species come many garden cultivars, some perennial, some grown as annuals, in a multitude of colors, bicolors, and combinations. They are often described as happy, cheeky, and mischievous, and like little boys of the same ilk, they never fall out of favor. Violas flower for long periods and are charming as edging and rock garden plants. They can also be used for bedding, as fillers in borders, and in pots, troughs, and hanging baskets.

GROWING NOTES

Generally more tolerant of heat and cold than pansies, violas will grow in most climates, with sowing, planting, and flowering times varying with location and cultivar. They will grow in full sun or half shade, and the degree of heat will determine which to choose. They are also tolerant of most soil conditions, but some added compost or manure never goes astray. *V. tricolor* needs little attention, but garden varieties will benefit from regular watering, especially if it is hot and windy; liquid feeding and removing spent blooms will lengthen the flowering period.

Opposite: The cheeky blooms of *V. tricolor* are simple and sweet.

Above left: A cultivar called Violetta Tiny Tots 'Blueberry and Banana'.

Above right: *Viola* sp.

VIOLA X WITTROCKIANA
PANSY

Many of today's most popular garden plants originate from the breeding efforts of English gardeners. Pansies are arguably the most popular of all annuals and we owe the development of them to two such amateur gardeners who, in the 1820s, began improving the native heartsease (*Viola tricolor*) (see page 154).

Since then, pansies have never gone out of fashion, and the recent advent of the giant varieties, with blooms up to 4 in (10 cm) across, has made them more popular than ever. There are more colors, mixes, strains, and series than those early breeders could ever have dreamed of. Seed houses choreograph mixes and medleys in ever richer or more dazzling colors. There are faced and unfaced blooms, pansies with plain colors, with contrasting eyes and edges, with stripes and blotches and velvety petals that may be straight or wavy or ruffled. The flowering time is generally late winter through spring, and into early summer in cooler conditions, although modern cultivars tend to have an extended flowering time in all climates.

GROWING NOTES

Pansies will grow in most climates and generally prefer full sun, but will tolerate semishade, especially in warmer climates. A well-prepared bed with fertile, organically-enriched soil that drains well provides the best possible conditions. There are no universal rules for sowing and planting, as it depends on the cultivar and climate, although pansies are generally sown or planted in the fall in warm zones and in spring in cool climates. The fine seeds are best started indoors. Remove some of the first flower buds to encourage larger flowers, and pick spent blooms regularly to encourage new flowers. Deep, weekly waterings will promote strong growth and good flowering, as will regular liquid feeds.

Opposite: *Viola* x *wittrockiana* Bingo Series.

Above: *Viola* x *wittrockiana* Bingo Series 'Lilac Cap'.

WARM

Warm colors are happy, bold, beautiful, and flamboyant. These refreshing colors stimulate and energize your mood. Warmth can imitate or reflect a climate, provide a tropical escape, or simply create a feeling of well-being. Warm colors appear nearer—perfect for making a large garden seem more intimate. Warm colors also make an entrance welcoming.

On the color wheel, red, yellow, and orange are the warm colors. When you combine the primary colors of red and yellow, shades of orange are created. Together, these complementary colors create a harmonious effect. Mix rust, deep maroon or burnt orange to turn the temperature down. Add lemon, apricot or cream pastels to lighten. Warm colors are enveloping.

Here we have blended annuals and bulbs that bloom primarily in colors of red, orange, and yellow. For other ideas, refer to the A to Z plant entries in "Multicolors." Enhance the feeling of warmth and vitality by blending in terracotta and champagne tones. For a vivid contrast, partner orange with blue, or yellow with violet; and add green foliage as a backdrop to red blooms.

ALTERNANTHERA SPECIES
JOSEPH'S COAT

Alternanthera is grown for its colorful foliage rather than its white flowers, which are inconspicuous.

It would be easy to fancy that the flamboyant foliage of these plants reflects the calypso and carnival of their native West Indies and Brazil. With green leaves that are blotched with yellow, orange, red, brown, copper or purple, *Alternanthera* has a host of descriptive common names, including calico plant, parrot leaf, copperleaf, bloodleaf, joyweed, and exhibition border. So we wouldn't be the first to be fanciful about *Alternanthera*. Some species are mat-forming, spreading perennials, but those grown as annuals are generally more upright, reaching around 1 ft (30 cm) high, although some grow considerably taller.

GROWING NOTES

Given their tropical origins, these plants do best in warm climates; the foliage is most colorful in full sun, although *Alternanthera* will tolerate some shade in very hot climates. Lower growers make decorative edging. *Alternanthera* are striking accent plants in containers, and they can also be kept as house plants, but they'll need good, light, moist soil.

AMARANTHUS SPECIES & CULTIVARS
JOSEPH'S COAT

L ike their relatives *Alternanthera*, these plants are generally grown for their exuberantly colored foliage. *Amaranthus tricolor* even shares the common name Joseph's coat, a reference to the vivid leaves that are blotched with various shades of yellow, red, pink, and copper. *A. caudatus*, with its descriptive common names love-lies-bleeding and tassel flower, is grown for its drooping, tassel-like panicles of blood red blooms. The tassels can be dried for arrangements, and indeed, the name *Amaranthus* comes from the Greek word for "unfading."

GROWING NOTES

These are plants for warm climates and sunny spots, although afternoon shade in hot summer climates is beneficial. They grow to 4 ft (1.2 m) so they need space too, although *A. caudatus* excels in hanging baskets, where its drooping flowers can be best admired. *Amaranthus* tolerate some dryness, and foliage color can be more vivid in poorer soils, which must drain well, as these zany plants are susceptible to fungal problems in wet conditions. *Amaranthus* should be planted with restraint if you want to avoid garishness.

Opposite: *Amaranthus* is grown for its exuberant foliage colors but should be used sparingly.

Top: *A. caudatus*, with its tassel-like flowers.

Above: The leaves of *Amaranthus* 'Joseph's Coat' are brilliantly blotched with various shades of yellow, red, pink, and copper, with the upper leaves often contrasting in color with the lower ones.

ANTIRRHINUM MAJUS
SNAPDRAGON

These two-lipped flowers are called snapdragon in English, wolf's mouth in French and lion's mouth in other languages because of their resemblance to the face of a beast, mythical or otherwise. Children delight in squeezing the backs of the flowers so that the mouths open and snap shut. This old-fashioned plant never goes out of favor, and although there are now varieties that have spikes of double or wide open flowers, it is the traditional varieties that remain perennially popular.

Colorful and versatile snapdragons come in different heights and can be used in the garden in a variety of ways.

There are many different varietal and series names, but snapdragons generally come in shades of bright pink, red, orange, yellow, and white, as well as bicolors. Taller varieties, up to 3 ft (1 m), are grown as cut flowers and look wonderful in mass displays and as fillers in mixed borders. Intermediate and dwarf varieties that grow to only 1 ft (30 cm) can be used for bedding and edging, or in pots.

GROWING NOTES

The species and cultivars are in fact short-lived perennials, but they flower best if grown from seed and treated as annuals. Snapdragons can be sown or planted almost year round in warm areas, except in the tropics, where they are best grown in

Perennially popular snapdragons can be grown in almost any climate.

winter or the dry season, for they are prone to fungal rust in warm, humid weather. In cold climates, sow seed indoors in the fall or early spring for setting out in late spring or early summer. Harden them off before planting in well-drained soil that is fertile but not too rich in nitrogen. They need full sun and a site sheltered from wind; tall cultivars may need staking. These plants are quick to flower. Pinch them out at about 4 in (10 cm) high to encourage bushy growth, and dead-head them frequently to prolong flowering time.

ARCTOTIS SPECIES & HYBRIDS
AFRICAN DAISY

The warm reds, oranges, golds, and yellows of *Arctotis* flowers are softened by the silver-green foliage. Some of the newer varieties have bronzy and wine-colored flowers.

African daisies grow in abundance on dry, sandy, and stony soils in South Africa, where they are also known as Monarch of the Veldt. Their broad and brightly colored, daisy like flower heads are generally orange, yellow or white with blackish central discs, attractively offset by the downy, silver-green foliage. Hybridizers have produced red, gold, purple, and pink forms, creating colorful additions to the plants we generally treat as annuals, although they will overwinter in mild areas.

GROWING NOTES

As with many plants, the natural habitat of *Arctotis* indicates how to grow it. These robust and spreading plants feel right at home on a warm, sunny bank, but are adaptable enough to be grown as a ground cover or to perform in a garden border, as long as the soil is light and sharply drained. Once established, they only need a moderate amount of water, but will benefit from regular applications of liquid fertilizer when in flower. In cool climates they can be grown as house or conservatory plants, but in the humid tropics they are best avoided.

BULBINELLA SPECIES
GOLDEN WAND LILY

Announcing their presence in late winter to early spring with spires of bright, usually yellow, star-shaped flowers, these striking plants provide vertical variety in a sun-drenched spot. Unfurling from the raceme, base first, are many tiny blooms; with long stems reaching 3 ft (1 m), bulbinellas such as *B. latifolia* (syn. *B. floribunda*) make excellent cut flower displays. Species include *B. gibbsii* var. *balanifera*, *B. robusta*, *B. augustifolia* and *B. hookeri*, which has edible fleshy roots. Bulbinella are often classified as herbs, and may flower in summer, depending on the species and climate.

GROWING NOTES
Tolerant of light shade, the majority of the 20 or so *Bulbinella* species originated in southern Africa, with six being from New Zealand; they are hardy to approximately 32°F (0°C). Grow these plants by dividing the rhizomes in the fall or by sowing seed during winter. In cold locations, sow trays in a greenhouse and place them outdoors in warmer weather. *Bulbinella* (a diminutive of the genus *Bulbine*) need good drainage and plenty of water during the growing period, but drier conditions during dormancy to prevent the roots rotting.

Opposite: Bulbinellas are also known as cat's tail and maori onion. Shown here is *B. robusta* 'Dancing Fawn'.

Above: *Bulbinella latifolia* (syn. *B. floribunda*).

CALCEOLARIA SPECIES & HYBRIDS
SLIPPER FLOWER

Subtle they are not, but *Calceolaria* have long been popular for an exuberant spring-flowering display.

Known as slipper flower, pocketbook plant and ladies' purses, these bushy annuals or biennials have rounded heads of clustered and curious pouched-shaped orange, red, and yellow flowers. You would not call these flowers subtle, for they even have veins, spots, mottles, and blotches to add to their impact. Popular since Victorian times but rarely grown in the garden, they are most often displayed under glass or as temporary indoor plants.

GROWING NOTES

These plants do not tolerate extremes of heat or cold. Although you can sow seed in the fall or spring, they are difficult to germinate and slow growing. So unless you like a challenge, it is easier to purchase plants from a nursery or florist. Greenhouse plants should be kept cool and airy but frost-free, while indoor plants should be placed in a well-drained potting mix in bright, indirect light. Water freely but never allow the soil to become soggy. Apply liquid fertilizer regularly.

CALENDULA OFFICINALIS
POT MARIGOLD

Flowers of the true marigold have been used as a herbal remedy since the Middle Ages, and as a flavoring for cooking pots since the Tudors. *Calendula officinalis* is still used in herbal preparations and as a colorful and edible addition to salads, but now we know it best as a garden plant. Indeed, pot marigold is one of the easiest annuals to grow and is useful for bedding, mixed borders, cottage gardens, and, of course, herb gardens. The many-petaled, daisy-like double flowers are traditionally deep orange and bright yellow, but gentler tones of cream, apricot, honey, primrose, and even tinged pink are available.

Pot or English marigolds are traditionally deep orange and bright yellow, but now softer colors are also available.

GROWING NOTES

Pot marigolds are easily grown in all but tropical climates in most soils, as long as the drainage is good. Full sun is generally best, perhaps with some afternoon shade in hot summer climates. Plants sown *in situ* in the fall will put on a late winter and spring display, but they can be planted in spring for flowering in cool summers. Remove spent blooms or cut them for vases to extend the flowering period.

CELOSIA ARGENTEA SYNS *C. CRISTATA, C. PLUMOSE*
COCKSCOMB

Above: Members of the Cristata Group feature bizarre wavy combs in many colors.

Opposite: Gaudy or gorgeous? Beauty is in the eye of the beholder.

We met some colorful members of the *Amaranthus* family earlier (see page 174), but they don't get any zanier than these. The erect plumes of members of the Plumosa Group, known as feathery amaranth and Prince of Wales feathers, are about as warm as it gets. When the taller types that grow to 2 ft (60 cm) are massed in public parks, you couldn't fail to notice them. There are semidwarf and dwarf forms that grow to only 6 in (15 cm), commonly sold in pots. The bizarre crested flower heads of the Cristata Group resemble a rooster's comb in colors that include orange, red, purple, and yellow. Both types are used in fresh and dried flower arrangements.

GROWING NOTES

Their colors and climatic preferences mean that celosias are best suited to tropical and warm zones, but they can be grown under glass in temperate areas, or started indoors and planted in a warm spot in summer. They will do best in full sun and in enriched and well-drained soil; potted specimens have been known to exist, despite total neglect.

COREOPSIS SPECIES
TICKSEED

Yellow flowers add cheer to a garden and *Coreopsis*, with bright daisy-like heads, are among the easiest to grow. There are perennial and annual species mostly native to the American prairies. The truly annual *C. tinctoria* is an upright, stiff-stemmed plant, which grows up to 3 ft (1 m). It has bright yellow flowers with dark red central discs. A number of hybrids have been derived from this species, some with double flowers. In cold areas, some of the clump-forming perennial types can be sown under glass or propagated from cuttings to grow as a summer annual in a warm, sheltered site.

GROWING NOTES

These adaptable plants will grow in almost any climate zone, even in infertile soils. In warm zones you can simply scatter seeds, for in fact they self-seed so freely you may need to stop them becoming naturalized by removing flower stems before the seeds ripen. This will also encourage them to continue blooming for a long period.

Opposite: *Coreopsis tinctoria*, also known as calliopsis, is an annual species and the parent of many hybrids.

Above: The cheeky yellow flowers of *Coreopsis* can be blended into many color schemes.

CROCOSMIA SPECIES & HYBRIDS
CROCOSMIA

Bringing a warm glow to summer-flowering gardens, crocosmia have brilliant spikes of red, orange or yellow flowers, some with tinted bronze hues or yellow throats, all with gladiolus-like leaves. Although the hybrid *C.* x *crocosmiiflora* is often classed as a garden escapee, cultivars varying in growth habit are often perfect garden specimens, such as the apricot-yellow-flowered *C.* 'Solfaterre': its bronze foliage has been awarded the prestigious Award of Garden Merit by the Royal Horticultural Society in England. Rich and red, *C.* 'Lucifer' has long been a popular garden variety, growing up to 4 ft (1.2 m) tall. A florist's dream, crocosmias are perfect for growing in pots.

In areas where this plant is a garden escapee, simply grow it in pots. Its tall stems make it perfect for cut-flower displays.

GROWING NOTES
Native to parts of South Africa with predominantly summer rain, some species are frost-hardy to 5°F (−15°C). Crocosmia enjoy full sun but species like *C. aurea* prefer dappled light. Plant them in moist, organic-rich, well-drained soil. Leave in the ground and divide every 2–3 years in spring. In cold areas, mulch over winter; in very cold areas, lift the corms in the fall and store them until spring.

CYRTANTHUS SPECIES

SCARBOROUGH LILY

Looking like a subtle version of its *Hippeastrum* relative, the small, scented, star-shaped flowers of *Cyrtanthus elatus* syn. *Vallota speciosa* bask in sunlit gardens. This scarlet form is the best known *Cyrtanthus*, widely grown for its cut flowers and as an indoor plant. However, most species look quite different, with fragrant, tubular flowers: *C. brachyscyphus* blooms are of red-coral; the exquisite *C. obliquus* has hanging yellow flowers edged with green; and the confusing *C. mackenii* (Ifafa lily) is supposedly white, with *C. mackenii* var. *cooperii* being yellow— and ivory, pink or apricot. Other species and cultivars have pink petals. Responding well to regeneration after bush fire is *C. ventricosa*, hence its common name of fire lily.

Opposite: *C. elatus.*

Above: *Cyrtanthus* may be evergreen or deciduous.

GROWING NOTES

Comprising around 60 species, native to southern Africa in mainly frost-free and summer rainfall areas, most *Cyrtanthus* bloom from late summer to mid-fall. There are only a few exceptions. Plant them so that the neck of the bulb is at or just above soil level. Divide the offsets in early spring, replanting immediately and watering in well. In cold, frost-prone areas, grow these plants in a greenhouse.

ERYSIMUM CHEIRI SYN. *CHEIRANTHUS CHEIRI*
WALLFLOWER

Naturalized in many parts of Europe and a cottage garden favorite since Victorian times, long-lasting wallflowers have a peppery fragrance. Although perennial, this species and its cultivars are treated as an annual or biennial, but they will overwinter in the right microclimate. Although flowers come in warm autumnal tones of yellow, orange, dark red, bronze, and brown, they in fact bloom in spring, or in late winter where winters are mild. The common name, wallflower, refers to the fact that these plants commonly grow wild on rocks, cliffs, and cracks in old walls and stonework.

Wallflowers grow 12–20 in (30–50 cm) tall and make lovely sweet-scented, spring bedding plants.

GROWING NOTES

Wallflowers grow in most cool to warm climates, except the tropics. Take a cue from their wild habitat, which shows they need sharp drainage and do best in moderately fertile, neutral to alkaline soil; add some lime if the soil is very acid. They prefer full sun but tolerate part shade. Sow seed from late summer or plant in the fall in warm areas, and provide winter protection in cold areas.

ESCHSCHOLZIA CALIFORNICA
CALIFORNIA POPPY

The natural habitats of this poppy-like flower are the hot, dry grasslands, coastal dunes, and inland hills of California, and it is the floral symbol of that state. The flowers have a satin sheen and are orange and yellow in the wild, but garden hybrids also come in vivid shades of scarlet, pink, carmine, mauve, bronze, and cream. The gray-green, feathery foliage is an added attraction. Some varieties have double or semidouble flowers, and sometimes frilled and fluted petals. These cheerful plants are charming in rock gardens, but look best when planted in large drifts.

GROWING NOTES

California poppy is a tough plant, for it is both drought and frost tolerant as well as totally unfussy about soil type, as long as the drainage is good. Although not suited to the tropics, it will grow in most other climates. The flowers close at night and in dull light, so they should be grown in full sun. As these plants are difficult to transplant, sow seed where they are to grow. They are likely to self-seed to provide bonus plants the following year.

Opposite: The flowers of California poppies have a satin sheen, offset by grey-green foliage.

Above: California poppy is an excellent annual for hot, dry gardens.

INDIAN BLANKET

The striking color combinations of *Gaillardia* flowers are set off by the fresh green foliage.

It matters not if the common name of these plants refers to the way the flower colors and patterns resemble blankets woven by Native Americans or to the fact that the wild species blanket their various North American habitats. We can simply appreciate the fiery tones of the red, yellow, bronze, and gold of their daisy-like flowers, which may be single or double and up to 5 in (14 cm) wide. There are annual and perennial forms, but since the commonly grown perennial hybrids *Gaillardia* x *grandiflora* are short lived, they are widely grown as annuals anyway, especially in warmer climates.

GROWING NOTES

These plants are easy to grow, their main requirements being full sun and good drainage. They enjoy dry summer heat and tolerate poor soils. *Gaillardia* can be sown *in situ* or planted in the fall or spring to bloom in summer through to the first winter frosts, or sown indoors in cold areas. The flowers are excellent for cutting; picking blooms or removing spent flowers will boost their long flowering season.

GAZANIA HYBRIDS
TREASURE FLOWER

Like so many other daisy-like plants from South Africa, gazanias have been extensively hybridized, becoming popular garden plants around the world. Although the hybrids originate from evergreen perennials, they are frost tender and best grown as annuals in cooler climates. They thrive on light, sandy soil, so are favorites in coastal gardens, windy sites, and banks, where they will act as a soil binder. Treasure flowers have felted, silver-gray foliage and a yellow, gold, orange, bronze, pink, mahogany or red flower, often with contrasting zones, which is also appreciated by birds, bees, and butterflies.

Warm, sunny colors are a gazania specialty. Many hybrids have stripes of contrasting colors.

GROWING NOTES
Low-growing and spreading, gazanias make good ground covers as well as colorful displays suitable for edging and in borders, rock gardens and containers. They flower for a long period through spring and summer, and will even do so in cooler climates in hot, sunny spots. They should be planted in full sun, for the flowers close in dull light. Avoid overwatering, as it can lead to root and stem rot.

GLORIOSA SPECIES & HYBRIDS
FLAME LILY

Gloriosa petals may bloom in different shades on the one plant.

L ike hot flames licking the air, *Gloriosa* climbs by leaf-tip tendrils towards the sun. *G. superba* is the single species from which all others are generally treated as named varieties. This striking tuberous plant has wavy-edged, brilliant yellow and red flowers; the hybrid 'Rothschildiana' has larger, strongly recurved crimson flowers with a yellow base. 'Greenii' and 'Lutea' are both yellow, while 'Carsonii' is purple-red with a lemon yellow edge and center. Blooming from late spring into summer in warm locations, later in cooler areas, these climbers need support as they can reach up to 6–8 ft (1.8–2.4 m).

GROWING NOTES

Gloriosa are best in tropical to near frost-free locations. Plant them from fall to early spring in a semishaded to full sun position. Mulch in frost-prone gardens or grow in a greenhouse or conservatory; plant after the last frosts. Considered an environmental weed in some locations (so ideally, grow it in pots), glory lily is poisonous if ingested. Keep the soil evenly moist during the growing season, reduce watering after flowering, and lift the tubers only during the dormant period.

GOMPHRENA GLOBOSA
GLOBE AMARANTH

Globe amaranth is a bushy tropical annual. The species and its cultivars are popular in tropical and warm gardens where they flower from summer into fall. They are also grown as florist's flowers for cutting and drying. Tall varieties growing to 2½ ft (75 cm) have been bred for commercial production, and there are also dwarf types to 6–10 in (15–25 cm), which are suitable for pots and edging. The pompon-like flower heads consist of papery-textured bracts that are magenta in the species but range through red, pink, purple, lilac, violet, orange, and white in the cultivars. The flowers maintain their vibrant color when dried.

An unusual plant for a tropical and warm climate garden, globe amaranth, also known as bachelor's buttons, is grown as a fresh and dried cut flower.

GROWING NOTES

As befits their tropical origins, these plants love heat and will tolerate drought and wind, but they can also adapt to all but very cold areas as long as they are grown in full sun and moderately fertile, well-drained soil. Sow seed from late winter to early summer in seed boxes or *in situ*.

HELIANTHUS ANNUUS
SUNFLOWER

Above: Plant sunflowers at the back of the border.

Opposite: 'Russian Giant' is the *Helianthus* for children to grow for a sunflower competition. It reaches 10 ft (3 m) or more.

Painted by Van Gogh, these striking plants provide seed for human and parrot consumption and for the manufacture of oil and margarine. The seeds are even used by quitting smokers as a natural remedy for nicotine craving. Children love to grow sunflowers, and their dramatic flower heads make excellent cut flowers. These, the tallest of all annuals, with huge flowers, just need lots of space, heaps of sun, and protection from wind. The 10 ft (3 m) tall varieties with golden yellow petals and dark brown or purple centers are the most familiar, but there are shorter cultivars and flowers with warm shades of bronze-red, mahogany-red, and creamy yellow.

GROWING NOTES

Sunflowers will grow in most climates, but do best where summers are long and dry. Simply plant the seed where the flowers are to grow. The richer the soil, the larger they'll grow. Those heavy stalks and droopy leaves absorb great quantities of water, so keep the roots moist by deep soaking; avoid overhead watering as these plants are susceptible to powdery mildew.

LACHENALIA SPECIES & HYBRIDS
CAPE COWSLIP

Prized by both enthusiasts for centuries, lachenalia was discovered in South Africa by plant hunters from the Dutch East India Company back in 1650. Often overlooked by gardeners, these winter- or spring-flowering plants with their spikes of tubular-shaped blooms are delightful in the garden or in a container. With around 100 species, new breeding work is producing many different cultivar shades (and with classification changes, species and variety names can be conflicting). Those commonly cultivated bloom in warm reds and orange (*L. bulbifera*), and in yellows, including the popular *L. aloides*, which is accented in red and green, with purple-striped leaves; 'Giant Aurea' is a larger, golden yellow cultivar. A few species, such as *L. arbuthnotiae*, are fragrant.

Grow Cape Cowslip indoors or for cut flowers. Other species and cultivars are shades of ultraviolet-blue, pink, and maroon. *L. aloides* is shown here.

GROWING NOTES
Originating in South Africa's winter rainfall climate, lachenalias enjoy plenty of water and good drainage in a sunny position or under deciduous trees; they are not fussy about soils, but light compost might enhance their growth. Protect them against frost. While they are dormant, refrain from watering them; repot plants grown in containers, thinning out the bulbs.

LIMNANTHES DOUGLASII
MEADOWFOAM

Above: Meadowfoam is also called poached egg plant for its distinctive white and bright yellow flowers.

Opposite: Meadowfoam looks delightful as an edging plant to pathways or borders.

Native to damp places and marshy meadows in western North America, meadowfoam make attractive cultivated plants in gardens. The low-growing, spreading plants bear masses of small, scented, slightly cupped white flowers with bright yellow centers, their distinctive appearance resulting in its alternative common name, poached egg plant. Its fern-like foliage helps make it a very attractive pathway or border edging; it also suits a rock garden, and is of course a candidate for inclusion in a meadow garden. Meadowfoam attracts bees, and although it has only a brief flowering period, it does self-sow, so will reappear each year.

GROWING NOTES
This is a plant for moisture-retentive soil. It dislikes extremes of hot or cold but grows easily where it has full sun and a cool root run in warm or cool zones. Sow seed where plants are to grow in the fall or spring, and make successive sowings to give a longer display.

LYCORIS SPECIES
SPIDER LILY

Named after the beautiful Roman mistress of Marcus Antonius, *Lycoris* are grown for their showy recurved petals and prominent stamens; they are often mistaken for their hardier nerine relatives. Generally their colors are yellow (*L. aurea*), creamy white (*L. albiflora*), and bright red (*L. radiata*, hurricane lily). The orange-petalled *L. sanguinea* is also called surprise lily, as it seems to appear overnight! *Lycoris* flowers bloom in late summer to early fall on bare stems, with the leaves emerging afterwards; there are a few exceptions, such as the rose-colored *L. squamigera*, or resurrection lily, whose foliage grows in spring.

For a complementary look, plant different species within the warm color spectrum. Shown here is *L. radiata*.

GROWING NOTES

Spider lily is best grown in cool greenhouses, or outdoors in warmer areas where little or no frost is experienced, although a few species are mildly frost tolerant. *Lycoris* don't like to be disturbed: potted specimens can be kept in the same pot for 4–5 years, while in-ground bulbs should be left in place. Depending on the climate, plant from late spring to late summer, in full sun or part shade. The bulbs make take several years to become established.

MIMULUS X HYBRIDUS
MONKEY FLOWER

Spots and blotches add impact to the already warm hues of monkey flowers.

The common name of monkey flower comes from the resemblance of the tubular flower with its flared mouth to the grinning face of a monkey. A very colorful monkey it would have to be, for these flowers are bright crimson, orange-red, yellow, burgundy, and pink, and many are blotched and spotted. Since they are among the few annuals that like to grow in cool, damp places, even bog gardens, and they don't mind shade, they are certainly a useful plant for providing warm hues in shady parts of the garden.

GROWING NOTES

Although a bushy perennial, *Mimulus* are usually grown as annuals, for they grow quickly from seed and are unlikely to survive either hot, dry summers or severe winters. Sow seed in trays in the fall or early spring for plants to flower in spring and summer. Monkey flowers will grow in pots and hanging baskets if they are given plenty of water.

NARCISSUS SPECIES
DAFFODIL, JONQUIL

The story from Greek mythology of Narcissus, who fell in a pond and drowned while admiring his own beautiful reflection, is well known—and who could resist admiring the exquisite flower named in his memory. This diverse range of cheerful spring and fall flowers has devoted followers—gardeners, bulb growers, mail order suppliers, nurseries, societies, clubs, and collectors. With over 13 000 hybrids available in all sorts of shapes and sizes, there's a plethora of colors and shades to choose from, including orange, red, apricot, pink, cream, white, and of course, yellow.

To distinguish these cold-climate plants, an official classification puts them into thirteen divisions (often based on a named species from which the hybrids are derived). This can also assist with selection and usage. The common name jonquil refers to *N. jonquilla* and its cultivars that usually have multiple, fragrant flowers, blooming late season and usually performing well in warmer temperatures.

Other scented cultivars include the Tazetta Group—with 3–20 small flowers per stem, good for indoors, containers, as cut flowers or for warmer climates—and the white-petaled Poeticus cultivars, with their green and/or yellow center and

Opposite: Just one of the many small-cupped hybrids displaying white petals and a colorful trumpet.

Above: The fragrant *N. jonquilla*, commonly called jonquil.

Above: *Narcissus poeticus* is commonly known as the poet's narcissus or pheasant's eye.

Opposite: The elegant *N. bulbocodium* or hoop petticoat daffodil.

red-edged cup. Excellent for rock gardens and pots are the Cyclamineus Group, with significantly reflexed petals and straight, narrow cups; the small-flowered Bulbocodium cultivars, commonly called hoop petticoat because of their drooping, pendent-like flowers; and the Triandrus Group, often with multiple blooms. The Split-coronas, also called Butterfly or Orchid daffodils, have trumpets that are split for at least one-third of their length.

If the trumpet or cup of the flower is more than one-third larger than the petals, they're called Large-cupped; less than one-third, they're Small-cupped. The often multiflowered Double has more than one ring of petals, while the Trumpet, probably the best known, has a trumpet the same length or longer than its petals. Wild Species are natural forms, species and hybrids (often good for rock gardens). Finally, the Miscellaneous Group is for all those that can't be placed anywhere else.

GROWING NOTES

Naricissus are easy to grow in fertile, moist, well-drained soil in cool climates. Some species and varieties are more tolerant of warmer conditions (except tropical), but the flowers are less reliable. Daffodils need chilly conditions for growth to start: in warm locations a spell in the refrigerator crisper may be sufficient. Plant in late summer (in cold climates) or in the fall (in warmer areas). Grow these bulbs in a sunny position or under deciduous trees with protection from wind.

Plant bulbs at least twice the depth of their length (pointed end upwards), allowing more depth in sandy soil than in clay. Space the bulbs of larger growers about 3–8 in (8–20 cm) apart; plant smaller types closer together. The bulbs multiply by offsets, and are often more productive after the first year. Dig up and divide *Narcissus* every three years or so.

Opposite: For best effect, plant daffodils in drifts or several clumps.

Above left: One of the many delightful hybrids of *N. bulbocodium*.

Above right: Grow small and multiflowered daffodils for spring- and fall-flowering gardens and as cut flowers indoors.

PORTULACA GRANDIFLORA
SUN PLANT

Above: *Portulaca* are drought-tolerant plants, making them an excellent choice for rock gardens.

Opposite: The clear, bright colors of *Portulaca* put on a dazzling display in gardens and cascading from hanging baskets and containers.

One of the few annual succulents, *Portulaca* are semiprostrate plants with cylindrical, fleshy, bright green leaves. The flowers are mostly double and rose-like, and they open only in the sun when their vivid, clear tones of pink, yellow, orange, red, magenta, and white put on a dazzling display. They originate from the dry regions of South America, so they are welcomed by gardeners with hot, dry spots such as banks, rock gardens, and the tops of dry walls that get watered only occasionally. Yet *Portulaca* are tough enough to grow in most climates, as long as they are planted in full sun and after the last frost.

GROWING NOTES
Portulaca seed can be sown in containers or *in situ* from early spring, and can be planted through spring and summer. This plant will tolerate any amount of heat and only irregular watering, and will grow in almost any soil, although they do best where it is sandy or gravelly, and relatively infertile.

RUDBECKIA HIRTA
GLORIOSA DAISY

This species is a biennial, but like a number of perennial *Rudbeckia* species, it is grown as an annual and will flower in the first year. The species has deep yellow, daisy-like flowers, with conical black or purple centers, that appear in late summer and fall in its native North America. Garden varieties produce big showy flowers up to 3 in (7 cm) wide in great profusion at a time when most other annuals have finished flowering. Some have color variations that include gold, orange, and fall shades, including bicolors. With new breeding there is now even a series with quilted petals. 'Prairie Sun', a recent prize-winning cultivar, has gold petals with lemon tips and chartreuse centers.

GROWING NOTES
Rudbeckia will grow in most climates in a sunny spot, in moist, well-drained, moderately fertile soil. Tall varieties that grow to 3 ft (90 cm) should be planted at the back of borders, but there are lower-growing varieties that can be grown in containers. Sow seed in early spring in trays under glass, or *in situ* in mid to late spring.

Opposite: Some *Rudbeckia* strains have bicolored flowers in red-brown, orange-bronze, and other fall colors.

Above: The combination of bright yellow petals and black centers makes *Rudbeckia* a striking plant in the late summer garden.

SALVIA SPLENDENS
SCARLET SAGE

The fire engine red flowers of scarlet sage are often seen in bedding schemes in public gardens.

The upright spikes of fiery red salvia flowers are beloved by municipal gardeners who want a bedding scheme of eye-catching color for a long period. Cultivar and series names such as 'Blaze of Fire' and 'Sizzler' indicate that these are truly hot plants. But in fact, the color range is more extensive than the familiar scarlet, and newer forms include purple, pink, salmon pink, and white. Although there are cultivars that grow to 20 in (50 cm), some reach only around 1 ft (30 cm), making them suitable for pots or as fillers in a mixed border.

GROWING NOTES

These are easy plants to grow in all but the coldest climates. In tropical warmth they may flower a second year, but in temperate climates they are raised as an annual under glass and hardened off, or sown *in situ*, or planted out when the weather and soil is warm. They will do best in a hot spot with full sun and will tolerate poorer soil, although good drainage and some added organic matter does improve performance.

SANDERSONIA AURANTIACA

CHINESE LANTERN LILY

Dangling pendulous, rich orange lanterns, the predominantly summer-flowering *Sandersonia* welcomes the start of the festive season in its native South Africa, hence one of its common names—Christmas bells. In the northern hemisphere, its flowers appear during July and August. *S. aurantiaca* is the only species. With a slightly climbing habit, this unique bloomer may grow to 3 ft (1 m) tall. Provide support for it in the garden or if you are growing it in containers. Due to its long vase life, *Sandersonia* is increasingly grown as a cut flower and export crop.

Chinese lantern lilies often need support for their slightly climbing habit.

GROWING NOTES
This plant prefers tropical to frost-free gardens. Add organic matter and ensure the soil drains well to avoid root rot. Grow it from seed or, more commonly, from its forked tuber. Lift and divide in the fall in frost-prone areas; store the tubers in a warm, dry place, and replant just before the last frost in spring. In warmer climes, plant in late winter or early spring; new growth will be produced from non-dormant tubers. In hotter climates, Christmas bells prefers a partly shady position with morning or afternoon sun.

SCADOXUS SPECIES SYN. *HAEMANTHUS*

PAINTBRUSH LILY

With prominent stamens and large, spherical umbels comprising 10–200 tiny star-shaped flowers, *Scadoxus* or blood lilies are striking spring or summer garden additions (although they may bloom later in some climates). Now botanically classed separately from their *Haemanthus* relatives, both may still be listed under the latter name in catalogues. These bulbous species include the most commonly grown red *S. multiflorus* and subspecies *katharinae*; dwarf paintbrush, *S. membranaceus*; and the royal paint brush, *S. puniceus*, with scarlet and yellow anthers. The leaves appear after or at the same time as these majestic blooms and produce shiny, often colorful, inedible berries after the flowers fade.

Above: Scadoxus multiflorus subsp. katharinae is named after botanical artist, Katharine Saunders. It usually grows to 1–2 ft (30–75 cm).

Opposite: Scadoxus multiflorus (syn. coccineus). Like most of the Amaryllis family, the bulbs of Scadoxus are poisonous if they are ingested.

GROWING NOTES

Native to South Africa and tropical Africa, *Scadoxus* are frost-sensitive and best suit tropical to near frost-free locations. In colder locations, grow them in containers indoors. Plant *Scadoxus* in humus-rich, well-drained soil; they are tolerant of semishade to even heavy shade. Water well during the growth period, then reduce during fall and winter (when some species are dormant).

SCHIZOSTYLIS SPECIES & HYBRIDS
CRIMSON FLAG

B old and red, *Schizostylis coccinea* add swathes of vibrancy to
borders, bog gardens, and stream or pond edges. Providing
welcome color during summer to winter gardens, the long-
stemmed flower spikes with their flat, cup-shaped petals are
excellent cut flowers. Looking like a miniature gladiolus, river
lily also belong to the iris family and are not lilies at all. The
heights of these plants vary, from 18 to 28 in (45 to 70 cm) tall;
the crimson-red hybrid 'Major' has larger blooms than the
species, while the red 'Viscountess Byng' is a late bloomer.
Although *S. coccinea* is the only species, hybrid varieties now
extend the color range to include pale pink, rose pink, salmon,
and white.

The long-stemmed flower spikes of *Schizostylis* make excellent cut flowers.

GROWING NOTES
As crimson flag originated in South Africa, it should be planted
in full sun or part shade in subtropical, cool or frost-free
gardens. In frost-prone areas, grow it in greenhouses until the
weather warms, or cover it for protection. The rhizomatous
roots form clumps and need to be divided every 2–3 years
during spring. Replant them in the garden or in containers.
Keep *Schizostylis* moist, particularly during the growing season.

SPARAXIS TRICOLOR
HARLEQUIN FLOWER

Above: These small flowers make colorful, compact container displays in a sun-drenched spot.

Opposite: *Sparaxis* are attractive border plants.

L ike jewels in the sunshine, the faces of these small blooms sparkle in the warm colors of red, burgundy, copper, yellow, and white. Most commonly available *Sparaxis* are *S. tricolor* (sold as 'Mixed'), which often bloom with a dark circle that separates the center from the colored petals, and despite its name, will also flower as bicolors. Some hybrids are available in purple, red or white. These small flowers are excellent as colorful, compact container displays, planted within borders or as rockery additions, placed in a sun-drenched spot. Blooming in late spring and summer, their long spikes of flowers will continue through to winter in warmer climates. With its sword-shaped foliage, this member of the iris family provides great cut flowers too.

GROWING NOTES

Native to South Africa, these plants may naturalize; depending on the location, some species are considered an environmental weed. *Sparaxis* need full sun with wind protection and well-drained soil. For best effect, plant corms en masse in the fall.

SPREKELIA FORMOSISSIMA
JACOBEAN LILY

Until a few years ago it was thought that the distinctive
looking *S. formosissima*—part of the *Amaryllis/
Hippeastrum* family—sat alone. But then a smaller species,
S. howardii, was discovered in southern Mexico. So far this new
addition isn't available from bulb suppliers. Blooming with
slender red, orchid-like petals, the Jacobean lilies may appear
during spring, summer or fall in the garden, or as showy
greenhouse or conservatory plants in cooler areas. Often
flowering before the strappy leaves appear, this *Sprekelia*
reaches 12–18 in (30–45 cm) in height, with each stem
producing one magnificent bloom, although larger bulbs may
produce more than one stem. There are limited named red
varieties available, but these are often just sold as the species.

S. formosissima is also
known as the Aztec lily.

GROWING NOTES
Originating in Mexico and Guatemala, these frost-tender bulbs
are planted in warm, frost-free climates during fall. In colder
areas, plant them after last frosts in spring, dig them up after
flowering and store in a cool, dry location. Jacobean lilies like
well-drained, organic-rich soils in a sunny, sheltered position.
Containers should be re-potted every three years.

STERNBERGIA LUTEA
AUTUMN CROCUS

Related to daffodils, but looking like crocuses, the clean, fresh yellow blooms of *Sternbergia lutea* brighten the front of borders and rock gardens in the fall. These small plants grow to 4–6 in (10–15 cm) tall, with narrow, strappy leaves of lush green that die back in spring. For best effect, plant bulbs in drifts and leave to naturalize. *S. lutea* can be grown in beds within a greenhouse or alpine house but it isn't happy in a container; in fact, it is best suited to outdoors. Other species and hybrids also have yellow flowers; with larger blooms, *S. candida* has white, scented spring flowers.

Above: For a cheery border, plant autumn crocus en masse. Make sure they receive at least dappled sunlight.

Opposite: *S. lutea* is commonly called winter daffodil, although it's not a daffodil at all.

GROWING NOTES
Autumn crocus originated in the limey soils of Mediterranean Europe, so are suited to cold, cool and near frost-free areas with hot, reasonably dry summers. Grow them in well-drained, fertile soil; they are tolerant of slightly acidic soil. Plant them immediately in summer, 8 cm (3 in) deep and 5 cm (2 in) apart, as these bulbs resent disturbance. Leave for 3–4 years before dividing. Grow autumn crocus in a sunny situation—in the northern hemisphere, the base of a south-facing wall is ideal; mulching is beneficial.

TAGETES SPECIES & HYBRIDS
FRENCH & AFRICAN MARIGOLD

French and African marigolds are among the most widely grown summer annuals. Despite their common names, both species are native to Central America and Mexico. The African marigolds, derived from *T. erecta*, are upright plants and their large, very double, pompon-like flowers up to 5 in (12 cm) across come in shades of yellow, gold, orange, and creamy white. Cream or vanilla flowers can be used to soften the hot yellows. There are tall strains—to 3 ft (1 m)—as well as intermediate and dwarf types, to 1 ft (30 cm). Tall marigolds are dramatic but they can look ugly if they are not well maintained; small to medium-sized marigolds are generally better for formal bedding or for growing in tubs.

French marigolds, derived from *T. patula*, are bushy plants and have daintier flowers that are usually double and carnation-like, although there are some single strains. Their colors and bicolors are fall yellows, rich orange-browns, and mahogany reds. Generally more compact than African marigolds, French marigolds are suited to mass planting and pots. Afro-French crosses combine the larger flowers of the

Opposite: Some French marigolds are single; they are often bicolored.

Above: The daisy-like, fully double heads of African marigolds can be as large as 12 cm (5 in) across.

Right: *T. patula*, a dwarf crested variety.

Opposite: African marigolds are available in various heights up to 3 ft (1 m) tall.

African marigolds with the more varied colors of the French ones. All have strongly aromatic, deeply divided, deep green leaves, and their summer and early fall flowers are suitable for cutting.

GROWING NOTES

These are among the easiest of annuals to grow, for they are fast growing, unfussy as to soil type, and suited to all but the coldest climates. They do need sun, well-drained soil, and regular deep watering, especially in dry periods and windy weather. African marigolds in particular need to be sheltered from wind. Mulch around the plants to conserve soil moisture. Regular applications of liquid fertilizer are beneficial, as is the removal of spent blooms. Sow either direct into the ground or into pots at various times, depending on type and climate zone.

TIGRIDIA PAVONIA
TIGER FLOWER

When choosing bulbs for colorful emphasis, don't overlook the intriguing, dramatic-looking tiger flower, also known as jockey's caps, peacock flower and Mexican shell flower. Similar in habit to daylilies, these spectacular blooms appear for one day only, but in succession to provide a long display. The most common *Tigridia* species available is *T. pavonia*, with its bright colors and shades of red, orange, yellow, purple, pink, and white on three large outer petals and three smaller inner ones. The blooms reach 4–6 in (10–15 cm) across, with blotched centers adding to their attraction. Growing in spring and dying back in the fall, they bring welcome color to summer gardens—earlier in some locations. For a stunning effect, mass plant mixed or single colors.

Red *Tigridia pavonia* looks stunning mixed with purple flowers.

GROWING NOTES

Tigridia originate in Mexico and Guatemala, and prefer subtropical to cool, frost-free gardens. These plants are not frost-hardy, so where winters are cold, lift during fall and store until spring. In slightly warmer areas, leave them in the ground and mulch for protection. Grow in full sun in friable, well-drained soil. *Tigridia* can also be grown from seed.

TITHONIA ROTUNDIFOLIA
MEXICAN SUNFLOWER

Above: Its gorgeous color makes *T. rotundifolia* well suited to tropical gardens.

Opposite: Mexican sunflowers are tall plants with flowers that are generally an interesting shade of orange-red.

Growing wild in Mexico, this member of the sunflower family grows stems up to 12 ft (4 m) tall. Fortunately, cultivated varieties aren't as lanky, although they can reach 5 ft (1.5 m). In late summer to early fall these long stems bear solitary zinnia-like flowers that are 2–3 in (5–8 cm) wide and generally a deep reddish orange, although there are yellow and scarlet varieties. The flowers attract butterflies and are good for cutting.

GROWING NOTES

This unusual annual is suitable for a hot, sunny garden and a warm color scheme. With its colorful flowers and many heart-shaped leaves, Mexican sunflower would be right at home in an exuberant tropical garden. But it will also grow in cooler climates if started indoors and planted out when it is warm. Because of its height, Mexican sunflower looks good at the back of a border and may require support. The soil should be well drained but need not be too fertile. The plants are drought tolerant once they are established.

TROPAEOLUM MAJUS
NASTURTIUM

Few plants are as easy to grow as nasturtium. It's simply a case of throwing the large seeds into the garden and waiting for them to grow—so easy, making nasturtium ideal for a child's plot—but make sure they don't become weedy in your garden. There are bushy and trailing types. Although the spurred, trumpet-shaped flowers are traditionally red, orange, and yellow, modern cultivars, which may be semidouble, come in rich velvety shades and softer, creamier colors, some interestingly blotched and bicolored. Both the flowers and the rounded leaves are edible, the leaves adding a distinctive peppery taste to salads.

Nasturtiums can be grown in any informal garden bed, on dry sunny banks. They are wonderful in hanging baskets and window boxes.

GROWING NOTES
Nasturtium will grow in all climates. Tolerant of dry conditions, it needs sun and good drainage, and prefers light soil, because if it's too rich, foliage will be produced at the expense of flowers. These plants will flower for a long period from spring to fall, especially if picked frequently, and may even flower over winter in warm climates. The large seeds sow themselves with abandon.

ZINNIA ELEGANS
YOUTH & OLD AGE

The strange common name of these old garden favorites refers to the way the new growth and blooms obscure old, faded flowers. Zinnias flower best in long, hot summers; in these conditions they put on a wonderful show when mass planted in the garden. The double or single flat-petaled flowers come in many shades of red, orange, purple, yellow, and pink, plus white. The solitary flowers are traditionally borne on long stems, although there are lower growing cultivars suitable for edging and growing in pots.

Above: Zinnias look best in mass garden displays and can be sown in succession for a longer flowering display.

Opposite: The flat-petaled flowers of zinnias may be single or double, and come in a wide range of warm colors.

GROWING NOTES

In tropical climates you can plant zinnias to bloom any time of the year, but in cooler climates wait until all danger of frost has passed. Since they dislike root disturbance, sow *in situ* if you can, or start indoors and transplant carefully. They need full sun, and the tall varieties require wind protection. Zinnias tolerate most soils as long as they are well drained. An open site with good air circulation will help prevent the fungal leaf diseases that can infect zinnias in humid areas.

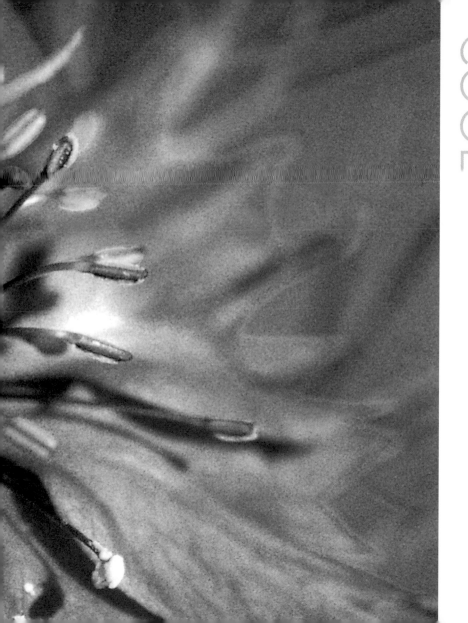

Blue and green instil calm, harmony, and peace; they bring a sense of relaxation and freedom to the garden. Blue is the foundation of cool shades and hues, reflecting the breadth of the sky. Cool colors appear to retreat, so when they're used in a small area, they give the illusion of more space and distance. Planted in a warm spot, they ease the temperature down.

Blue is cooling. It's a primary color—brilliant and enticing. Mix blue equally with red to make violet. If you shift the color balance, shades of purple and mauve are created. Plant with pastel colors for a soft, calming vision, and add white for a crisp look. To jazz up your garden, contrast blue with warm yellows, orange, and red. Add green as a natural, cool companion.

Assembled here is a smorgasbord of cool blues, mauves, and violets. Another cool color is green, and although this color is seldom found in the flowers of annuals and bulbs, foliage is a perfect substitute. Investigate "Landscaping: Using color" (see page 23) for ideas on harmonizing or contrasting the colors in your garden scheme. Pastels and white always make suitable companions.

AGERATUM HOUSTONIANUM
FLOSS FLOWER

There are pink and mauve-pink forms of *Ageratum*, also known as floss flower and pussyfoot.

The fluffy flower clusters of *Ageratum* come in a range of cool colors that bring calm to the summer garden and blend well with other flowers. Although the most common forms are powder blue or lavender-blue, there are also pink-mauve and white forms, and now even a red one. Native to Mexico and the West Indies, *Ageratum* is popular for summer bedding, edging, and containers in warm or tropical regions, but it will also tolerate temperate climates. Long-blooming, these plants keep a neat mounded shape through to the fall.

GROWING NOTES

Ageratum is easy to grow in a sunny location, or in partial shade in hotter climates. Plants do best in moist but well-drained fertile soil, but are moderately drought tolerant. There are tall—1 ft (30 cm)—to dwarf—6 in (15 cm)—types. Sow seed in trays or *in situ*. Plant out in late spring or all year round in warmer areas. Despite its virtues, *Ageratum* doesn't find universal favor: in parts of eastern Australia, for example, it is classified as an environmental weed and is given the name blue billygoat weed.

ALLIUM SPECIES & HYBRIDS
BALL-HEADED ONION

With many star-shaped flowers forming an intricate spherical mass, these onion relatives won't make you cry. Many ornamental species and varieties are available, including *A. christophii*, boasting a short stem but a big head; standing tall is *A.* 'Globemaster', with up to 1000 tiny florets forming its globe 8–10 in (20–25 cm) across. Opening green and turning a deep clover color is *A. sphaerocephalon*; easy to grow and commonly known as the round-headed leek, it's usually sold as 'Drumstick'. For best visual effect, plant ornamental onions in groups of odd numbers like three's. Look for rosy pink, mauve, cornflower blue, and white too.

GROWING NOTES
Blooming in late spring to early summer, alliums are best suited to cold and cool climates. Plant them in well-drained, sandy soil and full sun—they are great for gravel gardens, raised beds, and containers. Depending on the location, plant in the fall or early spring at a depth of 2–3 times the bulb diameter. Propagate by separating and replanting young bulbs; *Allium* can also be sown from seed.

Opposite: Each stem of *Allium giganteum* bears more than 50 lilac-pink, star-shaped flowers.

Above: *Allium christophii.* For something a little different, incorporate the spent blooms in dried flower arrangements.

BABOON FLOWER

Above: The fragrant blooms of *B. stricta* are also known as wine cup.

Opposite: When growing flowers that bloom in many different colors, for best effect plant en masse on their own.

Originating in the coastal habitats of southern Africa, where baboons dig up the corms for food, these low-growing plants with their ribbed leaves look similar to their *Gladiolus* relatives. Growing to only 1 ft (30 cm), *Babiana* have fragrant, brightly colored blooms in rich shades of blue, mauve, magenta, pink, and white; some are two-toned. The most commonly grown is *B. stricta*, or its hybrids, often sold as 'Mixed'; the freesia-shaped, tubular-flowered *B. plicata* has violet petals with a white or cream blotch on the lower lobes; and *B. rubrocyanea* is mauve, with a stunning red throat. Other species are also available.

GROWING NOTES

Best suited to warm, subtropical or Mediterranean climates with dry summers, *Babiana* is late winter-flowering in warm climates, spring-flowering in colder areas. Plant corms in late summer to mid-fall in well-drained, fertile soil in full sun or part shade. Check the recommended planting depth with the place of purchase as opinions vary greatly. Corms can be left undisturbed in the ground for several years, or dug up and stored over winter in cold climes.

BRACHYCOME IBERIDIFOLIA
SWAN RIVER DAISY

This dainty Australian daisy has found a place in gardens and hanging baskets around the world. The free-flowering plants form low, spreading mounds that become smothered in daisies in a variety of blue, violet, violet-pink, and purple shades plus white, often with yellow centers. These plants look best planted in large drifts, and are charming for edging, rock gardens, and dry, sunny banks, and in window boxes and containers of any sort. The finely divided, feathery foliage is an added attraction.

Brachycome are dainty daisies from Australia that form carpets of pretty flowers when mass planted.

GROWING NOTES

These plants will grow in a wide range of conditions, doing best in a warm, sunny, sheltered spot. The soil need only be moderately fertile, but well drained and retentive, for moist soil will help prolong flowering and the plants may die if the soil dries out. A good clip back in summer will maintain shape and promote flowering. In cool areas, sow seed under glass in late winter or early spring. Plants will self-seed in warm climates.

BROWALLIA SPECIOSA
BUSH VIOLET

The violet-blue petals and white centers of *Browallia* flowers attract attention when they tumble from hanging baskets.

The common names for this plant, such as bush violet and amethyst, indicate that it is the showy blue through violet to purple, white-throated flowers that make *Browallia* so desirable. There are also white-flowering cultivars. The shrubby annuals and perennials in the genus are usually grown as summer annuals in all but tropical areas. With its sprawling habit and many blooms, *Browallia* makes a pretty pot or basket plant, growing to about 1 ft (30 cm), but it can be grown in the garden as bedding, spaced 8 in (20 cm) apart.

GROWING NOTES

These are frost-tender plants, so in cool climates bush violets are grown as conservatory plants or house plants in good light. Outdoors, grow them in a warm, partially shaded position sheltered from drying winds in moist, humus-rich, well-drained soil. Pinch the shoots to keep the plants bushy, and avoid overfeeding, as it will result in extra foliage and fewer flowers. *Browallia* can be propagated from seed in spring and is commonly available as a potted plant.

CAMPANULA MEDIUM

CANTERBURY BELLS

Fortunately for the gardeners who cannot include the perennial bellflowers in their gardens, there are a few annual and biennial *Campanula* species; *C. medium* in particular will be familiar to fans of cottage gardens. Canterbury bells are a classic component of this garden style, and lend themselves to being massed in a mixed border or grown among shrubs. The upright spires, which grow to 3 ft (1 m) or more, bear masses of bell-shaped flowers in shades of blue, pink or white. The large-flowered double varieties lack the simple charm of the originals.

GROWING NOTES

This species is a frost-hardy biennial and does best in cool climates. It will flower in the first year if started indoors or if the seedlings are bought and planted in winter. It isn't suited to the tropics or hot, dry climates, but in warm temperate climates may even flower again the following year if the stems are cut after flowering. Specialist seed companies sell "annual" forms that don't require winter cold; these flower in the same season they are sown.

The large bell-shaped flowers of Canterbury bells appear in spring and summer, and look lovely in a mixed or annual border.

CENTAUREA CYANUS
CORNFLOWER

Such is the intensity of the traditional color of these thistle-like flowers that "cornflower blue" is a color description in its own right. Cornflowers or bachelor's buttons also come in many shades—of mauve, purple, violet, maroon, pink, and white—but none so beautiful as the original. As a wildflower in Great Britain and Europe, the original was once common as a cornfield weed, and has long been a component of cottage gardens. Bachelor's buttons are useful back-of-the-border plants and wonderful cut flowers. Flowers are usually produced on tall, gray-green stems growing to 3 ft (90 cm), but dwarf cultivars to 1 ft (30 cm) are also available.

GROWING NOTES

Bachelor's buttons are very easy to grow and best in temperate climates, and while they will tolerate frost and drought, they won't perform in tropical regions. They prefer full sun but will tolerate part shade. They are unfussy about soil type as long as the drainage is good. Sow seed *in situ* or plant in the fall or early winter in mild areas, or in spring where it is colder.

Above: The vibrant blue of these charming flowers looks wonderful in a mass planting.

Opposite: Tall-growing bachelor's buttons are excellent as background planting and for cut flowers.

CONSOLIDA AMBIGUA SYN. *C. AJACIS*

LARKSPUR

If you long to grow delphiniums but know that the climate will defeat you, here is your substitute. Larkspurs are true annuals, related to *Delphinium* and once classified as such, but they are not as tall. Their dense, graceful spires of blue, lilac, rose, salmon, and white flowers grow from 20 in (50 cm) to well over 3 ft (1 m), and are set among finely divided, feathery leaves. They are usually planted in a collectively cool array of mixed colors, and like their relatives, they are wonderful plants for cottage gardens, or the back of borders, blending with other annuals and bulbs. They are also good for cutting.

Larkspurs will flower in spring in warm areas, but in cooler climates they will bloom in summer and for a longer period.

GROWING NOTES

Unlike delphiniums, larkspurs will grow in cool and warm areas, but not in tropical regions. They are easy and fast growing if given rich, well-drained soil, full sun, and regular deep watering. Taller flower spikes may need staking and should be protected from wind. Larkspurs are not easy to transplant, and seed should be sown where the plants are to grow, in the fall in warm zones, spring in cooler places.

CYNOGLOSSUM AMABILE
CHINESE FORGET-ME-NOT

Cynoglossum amabile, shown here in spring with peach blossom and white Spiraea.

This plant self-seeds freely, whether it's between rice paddies or along roadsides in its native south-west China, or in gardens. But so attractive are its clusters of sky blue forget-me-not flowers and its gray-green stems and foliage, and so easy is it to remove self-sown seedlings, that it is a worthy addition to a garden, especially a meadow garden, and in warm areas where these plants will flower from early spring through to winter. Pink and white forms are also available. The cultivar 'Firmament' has pendulous flowers. Similar in appearance, the Cape forget-me-not, *Anchusa capensis*, is also worth growing as a blue-flowering summer annual.

GROWING NOTES

When a plant self-sows as freely as this one does, you know it must be easy to grow. The seeds form burrs and will stick to clothing, an experience that most people prefer to avoid. Simply place seed in sun or partial shade and in any type of moderately fertile and reasonably drained soil, and it is sure to grow.

DELPHINIUM HYBRIDS & CULTIVARS
DELPHINIUM

The majestic electric blue spires of delphiniums are the queens of summer borders and cottage gardens, but to be able to enjoy their royal largesse you need to live where there is a cool to cold winter. In warmer climes, don't so much as think about the herbaceous perennial types; even the Pacific Giant series, bred in California as short-lived perennials but usually grown as annuals or biennials, will be marginal. For those who can grow them, there are many named cultivars in shades of blue, purple, pink, and white. The Chinese delphinium, *D. grandiflorum* syn. *D. chinense*, is commonly grown as an annual and may give warm-climate gardeners some joy as bedding for one season. The flowers of the best known 'Blue Butterfly' are a gorgeous gentian blue, but these grow on loose branching spikes rather than on tall spires.

Opposite: *Delphinium grandiflorum* syn. *D. chinense* 'Blue Butterfly'.

Above: Delphiniums come in a range of cool colors but the deep blues are the most sought after.

GROWING NOTES
Delphiniums prefer full sun and well-drained, fertile, limey soil. The tall varieties need shelter from strong wind, even staking if necessary, as well as regular liquid feeding and watering to make those 5 ft (1.5 m) spires of flowers.

BLUE MARGUERITE

Southern Africa is home to a number of *Felicia* species, usually growing as sprawling perennials and evergreen subshrubs, but all bearing masses of small blue, daisy-like flowers, many with yellow disc florets. *F. amelloides* is the most widely grown in gardens around the world. These are perennial but not long lived, and as they won't survive winter frost, they are often grown as an annual or in a cool greenhouse. There are a number of true annual species, including the mat-forming *F. heterophylla*, with blue petals and centers, and *F. bergeriana*, the kingfisher daisy, with brilliant blue flowers that open only in sunshine.

Above: There are pink-, purple- and white-flowered varieties of *Felicia*, but it is the bright blue, daisy-like flowers that are the most common.

Opposite: Felicias bear masses of flowers for a long season, even all year round in warmer climates.

GROWING NOTES

Felicias are easily grown as annuals. They look particularly lovely in rock gardens and are good seaside plants; they can also be grown as bedding and in containers. They require sun but will grow in poor to moderately fertile, well-drained soil that should be allowed to dry out between waterings. Prune regularly to maintain shape and flowering, and propagate from seed or from cuttings taken in the fall.

HYACINTHOIDES SPECIES
BLUEBELL

Dangling petite trumpets from jaunty tall stems, bluebells are a welcome signal of spring's arrival. Flowering mid- to late-season, with a long display in cool areas, carpets of bluebells in woodland areas or drifts along borders in dappled light are sights worth waiting for. Bluebells are excellent for containers too. Traditionally grown are the delicate blue forms of *H. hispanica* (Spanish bluebell), reaching 1 ft (30 cm) tall, and the slightly smaller, upright *H. non-scripta* (English bluebell), a protected species in its native surrounds. Pink and white forms of both are available too.

GROWING NOTES

Bluebells are best suited to cool to cold climates; warmer locations and a sudden temperature rise in cold climes will produce shorter flowering displays. Plant bulbs 2 in (5 cm) deep and 3–4 in (8–10 cm) apart in late summer or early fall. These are easy-care bulbs; when they are overcrowded, divide them in late summer. Water bluebells regularly during the growth period, but reduce the amount of water during their summer dormancy.

Opposite: *Hyacinthoides hispanica*, or Spanish bluebell, naturalized.

Above: Although *Hyacinthoides non-scripta* has been reclassified, many suppliers list this and *H. hispanica* under *Scilla* and *Endymion*.

IPHEION UNIFLORUM & HYBRIDS
SYN. *TRISTAGMA UNIFLORUM*

SPRING STARFLOWER

Above: *Ipheion uniflorum* is a star performer when planted in rock gardens and pots with good drainage.

Opposite: Traditionally, pale blue is the common form but seek out other shades too.

Pointing their dainty, starry faces upwards, these bulbs are a must for mass planting, rock gardens, containers or alpine houses. With lightly fragrant blooms and strappy leaves that smell like onions when crushed, *I. uniflorum* are tolerant of poor growing conditions. Whitish blue is its normal color, with named varieties available. The popular 'Wisley Blue' is pale blue, while 'Rolf Fiedler' is bright blue; 'Froyle Mill' blooms almost deep purple; 'Album' and 'Alberto Castillo' are white varieties; and 'Charlotte Bishop' is a newer, pink cultivar. For a less vigorous bulb, try the yellow-flowered *I. dialystèmon*.

GROWING NOTES

Best suited to cool-climate, frost-free or near frost-free gardens, spring starflower will tolerate temperatures to about 14°F (–10°C), but a heavy layer of mulch is recommended. Reduce the depth of the layer as the weather warms up. Plant *Ipheion* 2 in (5 cm) deep and apart, in average soil. Bulbs will produce more prolifically after the first season or two. This plant has a prolonged flowering season from midwinter to spring, depending on the location; in cooler areas, flowers will appear later.

IXIA VIRIDIFLORA & HYBRIDS
AFRICAN CORN LILY

If you can't grow these delectable plants in your garden's conditions, move house! With spikes of jade green, star-like flowers on slender stems, green ixias put on a simply stunning display in spring or early summer. 'Viridiflora' means green-flowered, and these shimmering South African beauties also have purple-black eyes, adding to their graceful attractions. Reaching up to 3 ft (1 m), depending on climate, these plants can also be grown in pots in a cool greenhouse. More familiar are the smaller multicolored hybrids that bloom in warm and pink colors.

Ixia viridiflora has jade or blue-green flower spikes.

GROWING NOTES

Preferring a climate where gardens are frost-free or near frost-free, these bulbs can tolerate short periods of temperatures of 25°F (–5°C). In areas with heavy summer rainfall, *Ixia* are best grown in pots, as wet conditions may result in root rot. Plant in well-drained soil, or if you are growing them in pots, plant the corms in sand and a well-drained mix. When the plants are in flower, place them in a warm, sheltered position; keep them moist, but don't overwater them. Keep *Ixia* dry during the dormant season.

LIMONIUM SINUATUM
STATICE

Above: The papery blue or other colored calyces of statice retain their color when dried, but the white corollas fade.

Opposite: Although best known as a florist's or dried flower, statice is also grown in gardens. The mauve-purple shades bring some cool color to the summer garden, and can be cut and dried.

Walk on the seaside cliffs or dunes of the Mediterranean in summer and you'll see the papery blue flowers of sea lavender. This species or its near relatives grow wild in similar habitats in many parts of the world. Although it is an upright perennial, cultivated varieties derived from it are almost always grown as an annual and extend the color range to purple, mauve, magenta, pink, salmon, yellow, and white. They are grown in the floristry trade for fresh floral fillers and as dried flowers. The mauve-purple shades are most common in gardens. The tiny, papery, funnel-shaped flowers appear in clustered sprays or spikelets for a long period from spring to fall. They bloom on winged stems that arise from basal rosettes of foliage.

GROWING NOTES
Statice does best where summers are warm and dry, and of course it is excellent for seaside gardens. It needs full sun but any light, well-drained soil will suffice. Sow seed direct in clumps in the fall or early spring. It is slow to germinate and grow. Cut back plants after flowering to encourage new flowers.

LOBELIA ERINUS
LOBELIA

Profusely blooming lobelia can be seen as edging in gardens or cascading from window boxes, hanging baskets, and containers almost anywhere in the world that plants are cultivated. There are varieties with an upright or trailing habit, and some with dark, bronzed green leaves. It is the intense blue of lobelia flowers that makes them such popular plants, but the loose clusters of tubular, two-lipped flowers also come in violet, purple, rose, carmine, pink, cherry red, and white.

GROWING NOTES

Lobelia plants are easy to grow in almost all climates, for they are fast growers with a long flowering period. In cool temperate climates they will flower from spring to fall. In warm areas it is best to have them flower from late winter until early summer, for they do decline if the summers are very hot, yet they may well continue and overwinter if the conditions are right. They will grow in full sun or partial shade; humus-rich, moist, but well-drained soil will provide the optimum conditions. Water, liquid feed, and trim them regularly to encourage them through their long growing season.

Opposite: It is the intense deep blue of of Lobelia that accounts for their universal popularity.

Above: There are many varieties in a wide range of colors.

LUNARIA ANNUA
HONESTY

Despite its botanical name, honesty is in fact a biennial. It is a dual-purpose plant, grown for its violet-purple and sometimes white flowers, and for its circular, silvery, translucent seed cases that seem to resemble coins. Although the blooms are useful as cut flowers and bring cool color to shady settings, it is the delicate seed cases that have been popular in floristry and dried flower arrangements since Victorian times. The pointed, oval leaves have serrated edges and are sometimes variegated.

GROWING NOTES
Honesty prefers cool climates but will grow and self-seed almost anywhere, making it excellent for woodland or wildflower gardens as well as cottage gardens. It is most valuable for a moist but well-drained spot in part shade, but will also grow in full sun and tolerate occasional drying out. For dried arrangements, cut honesty when the pods are mature and dry, and hang the cuttings upside down in a dry, airy place until you can remove the outer skin of the pod.

Top: The seed cases of honesty are green before they turn translucent.

Above: The silvery seed cases are popular for dried flower arrangements.

Opposite: Honesty flowers have a luminous quality that is appealing in shady settings.

LUPINUS HARTWEGII
LUPINS

Here we meet another genus in which the showiest members are perennials suited only to climates with a frosty winter. Warm-climate gardeners must forgo the handsome Russell hybrids and be content with the annual *L. hartwegii*. These fast-growing bushy plants have hairy leaves and slender flower spikes to about 28 in (70 cm). The pea-like flowers are usually grown as a mix of colors in pale, cool tones of blue, mauve, pink, and white. They look best planted as a mass display but can also be mixed with other annuals or perennials. Their distinctive, peppery scent is most apparent in warm weather. Other annual lupins include *L. texensis*, Texas bluebonnet, and *L. nanus*.

Annual lupins aren't as showy as their taller perennial cousins, but they look attractive in mass plantings and are excellent for cutting.

GROWING NOTES
Full sun is a must-have but rich soil and added fertilizer aren't necessary, as these are leguminous plants that fix nitrogen in their root nodules. However, the soil should be well drained and lightly limed if it is on the acid side. In mild areas, sow seed in the fall where the plants are to grow.

MOLUCELLA LAEVIS

BELLS OF IRELAND

Here is an annual for those who love green flowers. Actually, the true flowers are fragrant, tiny, and white, and deep in the center of the papery green bells formed by the calyces. Another curiosity is that these plants originate on the stony slopes of Turkey, Syria, and Iraq; the Irish reference only relates to their green color. They'll grow in a wide range of climates and are useful for cutting and drying. The flowering period is short, but they last well if picked when the flowers are well formed. Remove the prickly-textured leaves from the stems so that the bells become more conspicuous.

The actual flowers of the bells of Ireland are the tiny, white bits in the center of the papery green bells of the calyces.

GROWING NOTES

The flower spires of these plants grow to 3 ft (90 cm), so they require wind protection and staking if necessary. Deep watering will encourage a good root mass to support the plants. Bells of Ireland will grow in sun or light shade and need moist, well-drained soil, preferably enriched with organic matter. They will self-seed, and should be sown *in situ* after danger of frost has passed.

MUSCARI SPECIES
GRAPE HYACINTH

With small clusters of flowers resembling bunches of upside-down grapes, *Muscari armeniacum* is an easy-care old favorite. They naturalize easily under deciduous trees or shrubs, and their fragrant blue blooms delight gardeners. Grape hyacinths are excellent for containers or rock gardens, as well as indoor forcing. Although there are many different species of *Muscari*, this is one of the half dozen commonly cultivated, with cobalt blue being the traditional color. Other varieties boast varying shades of blue; look out also for the white and double-flowering varieties. *M. azureum* is more open; *M. latifolium* is two-toned; and the tassel hyacinth (*M. comosum* 'Plumosum' syn. *Leopoldia comosa*), is mauve-pink and feathery.

Opposite: The flowers of *Muscari armeniacum* have white mouths.

Above: Plant grape hyacinths with a warm color, such as the yellow of daffodils, to enhance blue tones.

GROWING NOTES
Muscari is best suited to cool to cold climates but will tolerate warmer areas; it is not suitable for the tropics. Plant bulbs 2 in (5 cm) deep and 2–3 in (5–8 cm) apart in late summer or early fall. The flowering times vary between species and varieties from early to late spring. Some *Muscari* may be invasive. Divide grape hyacinth every 3–4 years, or lift and store until fall.

MYOSOTIS SYLVATICA
FORGET-ME-NOT

Above: Forget-me-nots are very pretty additions to garden borders.

Opposite: Forget-me-nots are traditionally planted beneath spring bulbs and other flowers, as shown here with *Primula obconica* and *Babiana*.

May-flowering tulips underplanted with dense carpets of forget-me-nots are a traditional feature of the English garden, but *Myosotis* are equally lovely when grown in dappled sunlight under deciduous trees, where they will flower for weeks on end. But they won't look out of place in rock gardens, as edging beside paths, and in garden borders. The plants form ball-shaped mounds about 10 in (25 cm) high, and the tiny flowers are traditionally sky blue with yellow centers, but there are also pink and white varieties, and all can be used to complement other plants with stronger color and form. And don't forget to cut some, for they will last well as cut flowers and are so pretty in small bouquets.

GROWING NOTES

Frost-tolerant and heat-sensitive, forget-me-nots do best in cool climates, but can also be grown in warm regions, except for the tropics. They thrive in moist, semishaded situations with a little morning sun and soil with high organic content, and where they do thrive, they usually self-seed freely.

NEMOPHILA MENZIESII SYN. *N. INSIGNIS*
BABY BLUE-EYES

In its native California, this low-growing, spreading annual grows on moist slopes and grassy flats. In cultivation, plants bloom prolifically and for a long period. The shallow cup-shaped flowers are china blue with a white center, making them a lovely component of a two-toned border edging or partner in a spring bulb display. They are also suitable for rock gardens, window boxes, and containers. The cultivar 'Pennie Black' has deep purple to black flowers and a scalloped, silvery white rim. *N. maculata* or five spot has long-stalked white flowers with a violet-blue blotch on the tip of each of its five lobes.

Opposite: The china blue and white-centered *Nemophila* is one of the loveliest of annuals.

GROWING NOTES

These are easily grown plants that like a fertile, moist, well-drained soil in a cool, partly shaded position in hot areas, although they will take full sun in cool districts where they will grow best. Baby blue-eyes will not tolerate heavy clay soil and may not survive dry summer heat, so should be watered freely in hot, dry conditions. Sow seed *in situ* in the fall or early spring in cooler areas. *Nemophila* self-sows freely.

Above: Here *Nemophila* intermingles with another charming annual, *Limnanthes*, or meadowfoam (page 212).

RESEDA ODORATA
COMMON MIGNONETTE

Cultivated in France for its essential oil, this old-fashioned plant wouldn't be given much garden room if it weren't for its intensely sweet perfume. It has weedy-looking leaves and tiny flowers that may be white, greenish, yellow-green, inconspicuous pink, coppery red, or variations on these themes. The flowers are born in conical heads on 1–2 ft (30–60 cm) stems from late winter to early spring in warm zones, summer to early fall in cool areas. Tuck it among other plants where the fragrance can be appreciated, and use it as a fresh or dried cut flower.

It wouldn't win any beauty awards—mignonette is grown for its intensely sweet perfume.

GROWING NOTES
Mignonette grows naturally in the scrub and stony hills of North Africa, which indicates that it likes well-drained soil that is neutral or slightly alkaline, so add lime if necessary. It will grow in most climates and will tolerate sun or part shade, but it needs full sun to bring out its scent. Water mignonette regularly, but don't let the soil become soggy. Sow seed *in situ*, pinch out the tips to encourage branching, and dead-head to prolong flowering.

SALVIA FARINACEA
LAVENDER SAGE

The huge *Salvia* genus comprises over 900 species of annuals, perennials, and soft-wooded shrubs. All bear upright spikes of tubular two-lipped flowers, and most have aromatic leaves; many of these are used as culinary herbs, while some have medicinal properties. Indeed the botanical name derives from the Latin *salvus*, meaning "safe" or "well." We have already met the warm reds and purples of *S. splendens* (see the entry in "Warm," page 228), but *S. farinacea*, with its slender spikes of densely packed, lavender-like flowers in deep purple-blue or white, looks quite different and adds a cool element to summer borders. Lavender sage can be used as bedding or for mass display, and the flowers are suitable for cutting.

Salvia farinacea is easy to grow. Its purple-blue flower spikes look best in a mass planting.

GROWING NOTES

Salvia farinacea will overwinter in warm areas, but it is commonly grown as an annual. Sow or plant it in the fall or spring, depending on the climate. It will grow in full sun and tolerates hot, dry weather, but will enjoy some protection from afternoon sun in hot climates. Pinch young plants to promote bushiness and cut back hard in mid-fall to encourage it to overwinter and re-shoot the following spring.

SCABIOSA ATROPURPUREA
PINCUSHION

There are a number of pincushion species with similar flowers, and *S. atropurpurea* is variously described as an annual, a biennial, and a short-lived perennial. But whatever its classification, it's certainly worth growing. The plants are upright and bushy with lance-shaped, lobed leaves. The flowers, borne on slender stems from summer through to early fall, are lightly scented, dome-shaped and 2 in (5 cm) across, and come in a range of cool shades of pink, red, blue, purple, and white. Lovely as cut flowers, *Scabiosa* are good for cottage and wildflower gardens, and for filling between shrubs.

GROWING NOTES

Pincushion flowers will grow well in most climate zones if they are given sun and moderately rich, well-drained, alkaline soil. Sow or plant *Scabiosa* in the fall, or in spring in warm areas. Regular, deep watering in dry weather (avoiding wet feet), liquid feeding, and picking or removing dead blooms will encourage continual flowering.

Opposite: Pincushions are shown here in a cottage-type planting.

Above: The cool colors of pincushions mingle well with those of other plants in many types of gardens.

SCILLA PERUVIANA
GIANT SQUILL

The multitude of intensely deep blue starry flowers with yellow anthers open successively to produce a stunning display during early summer. With near-evergreen strappy foliage, the giant squill makes an excellent container plant with long-lasting flowers, although its flower color may vary to include white. There are around 90 species of scilla. The genus is worthy of further exploration by novice or inquisitive bulb growers looking for more blue flowers; one of them is the dainty, easy-to-grow *S. siberica*, which is suitable for frost-prone locations.

Despite its name, *Scilla peruviana* originates in southern Spain, and is related to hyacinths, grape hyacinths, and bluebells.

GROWING NOTES
Although giant squill is best suited to a Mediterranean climate, it can be grown in a cool greenhouse in cool temperate climes, where temperatures are below 25°F (–5°C). Plant it in well-drained soil or raised beds, during fall, in full sun or partial shade, so that the bulb neck is just above soil level. This plant needs to be kept reasonably moist during the growing period, but during the winter dormancy it should be kept dry. Propagate from seed or by dividing offsets in late summer to early fall.

SENECIO CINERARIA SYN. *SENECIO MARITIMA*
DUSTY MILLER

This evergreen subshrub, which grows to 1–2 ft (30–60 cm) high, is widely grown as an annual for its silver-gray foliage rather than for its mustard yellow, daisy-like flowers. These plants form neat mounds of finely divided, lacy leaves covered in white hairs, giving them a silver-dusted effect. Dusty miller is often grown to provide color contrast in formal bedding schemes or as edging design, but it is also effective in informal or cottage gardens or as added color in container plantings. The foliage looks good in cut arrangements.

The flowers of dusty miller are usually removed to encourage leaf growth.

GROWING NOTES

This is an easy-to-grow plant that thrives in many climates and conditions, including heat and salt air, but not humid, wet conditions. It must have full sun and well-drained soil, but will tolerate poor soil. Like many silver-leaved plants, it is drought tolerant, so water regularly until the plants are established, then provide only a good soaking once a week. Dusty miller can be sown directly in the garden or rooted from cuttings of the firm, central growth.

PINK

Pink is a vibrant color—sassy, shocking, daring, even hot. Jazz up a quiet area with splashes of brilliance. Fill your garden with joyful exuberance. Alternatively, seek out its shy and alluring alter ego and blend softer pink tones and shades for a quieter effect. Create a romantic and feminine garden with rosy pinks, pastels, and white.

Pink is magenta, cerise, salmon pink, and rose. Pink is a blend of red, a primary hot color, and a nearby secondary cool color hue, such as indigo or violet. It's also the result of red and white. Create drama by combining pink with deep blue and mauve or red; or blend pink with pastels for a subtle scheme. Enrich pink by accompanying it with white.

As pink can be classed as either a hot color with red at its base, or a cool one with blue being more predominant, we've given this color its own chapter. Select the right tone or hue to suit your color scheme. Mass plant one pink color with complementary colors, or intersperse it with neutrals. Choose yellows carefully, selecting a comfortable companion.

AGROSTEMMA GITHAGO
CORN COCKLE

The fact that this fast-growing Mediterranean native has become naturalized in many parts of Europe, and was once commonly found in cornfields, tells you that corn cockle is ideal for summer meadow gardens or wildflower borders in cool to warm areas. The upright, hairy plants also create charming swathes in cottage gardens or beds and borders, although their 2–3 ft (60–90 cm) stems make them more suited to the back of the border. They bear large, open, trumpet-shaped, lightly veined flowers. 'Milas', the most common variety, has soft magenta pink blooms. Other shades of pink and white forms are available too.

Above: 'Milas Cerise' has cerise pink flowers.

Opposite: Corn cockle flowers are suitable for cutting, but the tiny seeds are poisonous.

GROWING NOTES
Sow seed in early spring or fall where the plants are to grow. Close sowing will help the rather flimsy plants support each other, although they may require additional support. They need full sun, and well-drained, not too fertile soil. They tolerate hot, dry summers once they are established, and dead-heading will prolong flowering. Self-seeding should be prevented in areas where they may become weeds.

AMARYLLIS BELLADONNA & HYBRIDS
NAKED LADY

Sweetly scented flowers borne in bunches on tall, naked stems bring welcome color to gardens during fall. The botanic name of this South African bulb is often confused with a common name used for *Hippeastrum*, which has larger flowers and a hollow stem, and is grown primarily as an indoor plant in cool locations. *Amaryllis belladonna*, however, has softer-looking blooms, usually of pale pink and white, with hybrids available in various shades of pink, from carmine to rose; 'Hathor' is white with a yellow throat.

Opposite: The delicately fragrant blooms of a belladonna lily.

Above: *Amaryllis belladonna* puts on a bold garden display during fall.

GROWING NOTES

Belladonna lily is best suited to subtropical, frost-free and near frost-free gardens; in colder locations, plant bulbs against a sun-drenched wall, approximately 4 in (10 cm) deep, and mulch for protection. In warmer areas, plant bulbs with their necks at soil level. Grow *Amaryllis* in organic-rich, well-drained soil in a sunny location, in partial shade in hot climates. For the best results, leave the bulbs undisturbed for several years. Plants can also be grown successfully in containers, in a quality mix; in colder locations, house in a cool greenhouse.

BELLIS PERENNIS
ENGLISH DAISY

This is one of the few annuals that are commonly referred to by their botanical name, although its common name reflects its quintessential Englishness. While the Latin name tells us this plant is perennial, and it will perform as such in a cool summer climate, it is commonly grown as an annual. The garden varieties are a far cry from the wild English original, some having fluffy, usually double flowers, many having quilled button- or pompon-like petal arrangements. Suited to bedding, edging, rock gardens, and containers, these ground-hugging, neat plants grow to 4–6 in (10–15 cm). The flowers come in shades of pink, rose, red, salmon, and white, as well as in bicolors.

GROWING NOTES

Cool temperate climates are best for these plants, even when they are grown as annuals. They are usually sown in trays indoors, or outdoors in seedbeds in late summer or fall, and hardened off and transplanted to flower in late winter or spring, depending on the location. English daisies will grow in full sun or semishade in almost any garden soil, but they will benefit from added organic matter and mulch to retain moisture.

Above: English daisies make neat, low-growing edging plants.

Opposite: *Bellis perennis* come in shades of pink, rose, red, salmon, and white, and in bicolors.

BLETILLA STRIATA
HARDY ORCHID

With miniature orchid flowers perched on wiry stems, these temperate ground-dwellers are easy to grow in a woodland garden, greenhouse or in containers. With about ten species within the genus, *B. striata* is one of the most popular, with its cattleya-like petals borne on stems 12–15 in (30–38 cm) tall. Blooms of magenta pink appear in spring or summer. Their iris-like pleated leaves provide attractive-looking foliage too. These plants are often listed with specialist bulb suppliers and orchid growers; hunt around for the pure white form and the white-edged variety.

GROWING NOTES

Best suited to temperate locations, Chinese ground orchid is hardy if it is protected from severe frosts. Grow it in sheltered areas with other plants, such as hardy ferns and trilliums; it is tolerant of both sun and dappled light. Plant pseudobulbs 2 in (5 cm) deep (or deeper in cold climates) in damp, humus-rich soil, during spring. *Bletilla* are best left undisturbed for 3–4 years before being divided in spring.

Opposite: Growing from pseudobulbs, *Bletilla striata* is best suited to areas with a temperate climate.

Above: *B. striata* is also known as the Chinese ground orchid.

CATHARANTHUS ROSEUS SYN. VINCA ROSEA
VINCA

Madagascar periwinkle or vinca flowers resemble *Impatiens* blooms.

Often confused with the true European *Vinca*, this tropical plant from Madagascar has given rise to a number of garden forms that can be grown as evergreen perennials in warm climates but are commonly used as annuals for bedding, borders, and pots elsewhere. The open, five-petaled flowers are in tones of pink and rose and also mauve and white, usually with a darker central eye. Modern breeders are developing trailing types.

GROWING NOTES

These are heat-loving and drought-tolerant plants, but they are not cold tolerant, so while they grow with abandon in tropical areas or as summer bedding in temperate zones, where they will tolerate both hot sun and partial shade, they are conservatory or house plants in cooler climates. Moist but well-drained, compost-enriched soil is recommended, as is tip pruning to encourage bushiness. Propagate *Vinca* from seed or cuttings.

CLARKIA AMOENA SYNS GODETIA AMOENA, GODETIA GRANDIFLORA, C. GRANDIFLORA
GODETIA

Pink can mean many shades, and the upright, cup-shaped flowers of godetia come in many hues of red, pink, crimson, salmon pink, carmine, and white. Native to north-western North America and named after a famous explorer of that region, godetia is also known in Europe as "Farewell to Spring" because it is the last of the spring annuals to come into bloom, making it useful for bridging the gap between spring and summer flowers, especially in the cut-flower trade. Many annual species grow in the wild, but the garden hybrids of C. amoena are the most commonly cultivated. They vary in height, and the blooms may be single or double, with ruffled and frilled petals, some resembling azaleas.

Godetia comes in many shades of pink and looks good mass planted. It is excellent for cutting.

GROWING NOTES
Godetia does best in cool or temperate regions, and is unsuited to very hot or humid areas. It is a sun-loving plant that prefers dry conditions, so plant it in a sunny position in light, slightly acid soil with perfect drainage. Sow in situ in the fall or spring as it dislikes being transplanted.

COLCHICUM AUTUMNALE
AUTUMN CROCUS

Above: Autumn crocus is also known as meadow saffron and naked ladies.

Opposite: Although autumn crocus is used in homeopathic medicine, all parts of the plant are poisonous if ingested.

The common name, autumn crocus, is misleading as the traditional, true crocus flowers in spring. *Colchicum fallale* is a crocus relative with blooms that appear in the fall on tall stems, long before its leaves. The species has soft pinky white petals, with a white hybrid called 'Album'. Perfect for borders, naturalizing, raised beds, and rock gardens, autumn crocus can look untidy in containers. This wide genus consists of around 45 species (including *C. speciosum*, *C. byzantinum*, *C. agrippinum*, and the spring-flowering yellow *C. luteum*) and various hybrids in shades of pink, purple, and white. Flowering times vary too, with spring and summer bloomers. Popular cultivars include 'Waterlily', with its pink, double, nymphaean-like petals, and 'The Giant', with its large lilac-pink flowers.

GROWING NOTES

C. fallale grows best in cool to cold climates, being hardy to −4°F (−20°C). Other species that originated in Mediterranean areas will tolerate warmer conditions. Plant corms in groups 4 in (10 cm) deep and 4–8 in (10–20 cm) apart, in mid to late summer. Autumn crocus needs well-drained, moderately fertile, moisture-retentive soil.

CRINUM X POWELLII
CAPE LILY

Blowing their own fragrant trumpets, the large, pink blooms of *Crinum x powellii* are bold and showy during late summer or fall in warm gardens. In cooler locations, they create a dramatic pot display indoors, within a greenhouse or a conservatory. With long stems bearing clusters of abundant blooms, plants can reach heights of 2–4 ft (60–120 cm); allow room for their strappy foliage spread. 'Album' is a popular white variety. Explore other species and hybrids, including *C. bulbispermum* and *C. moorei.*

Scented *Crinum x powellii* bloom on tall stems, and are ideal for planting in pots, near a window or in an outdoor seating area that is protected from strong winds.

GROWING NOTES

Suited to tropical, subtropical and temperate conditions, Cape lily bulbs should be planted in humus-rich and moisture-retentive soil, with their necks just above ground level. In cold locations, mulch to protect the bulbs from light frosts. Plant in full sun to partial shade, depending on the climate; in hot areas provide morning sun, and in cooler locations in the northern hemisphere, plant bulbs against a south-facing wall. Leave for several years before dividing, as these bulbs resent being disturbed. All parts of these bulbs are poisonous if ingested.

DIANTHUS SPECIES, CULTIVARS, & HYBRIDS
CARNATION

Above: The fragrant flowers of Sweet William come in pink, red, burgundy and white.

Opposite: Various *Dianthus* species planted with snow-in-summer.

This large genus has been cultivated for centuries and has some interesting associations. *Dianthus* means the "flower of Zeus or Jupiter," and was regarded as sacred by the ancient Greeks. Although pink is the dominant flower color, the name actually refers to the serrated petals that appear to have been shaped by pinking shears!

D. barbatus, Sweet William, has been a popular English cottage garden plant since the 16th century. Traditionally grown as biennials, several varieties flower readily the first year from seed. There are many cultivars, usually with flattened heads of fragrant flowers, some with double flowers that may be red, pink, purple or white, often two-toned. They may be used as fillers in a border or planted en masse, and are good cut flowers.

Slow-growing and compact, *D. chinensis*, the Chinese or Indian pink, has tufted gray-green foliage and loose clusters of slightly scented, single or double flowers in shades of pink, red, lavender, and white. It is suitable for edging and for troughs and window boxes. *D. caryophyllus* is the ancestor of the perennial florist's carnations, and also of the annual or

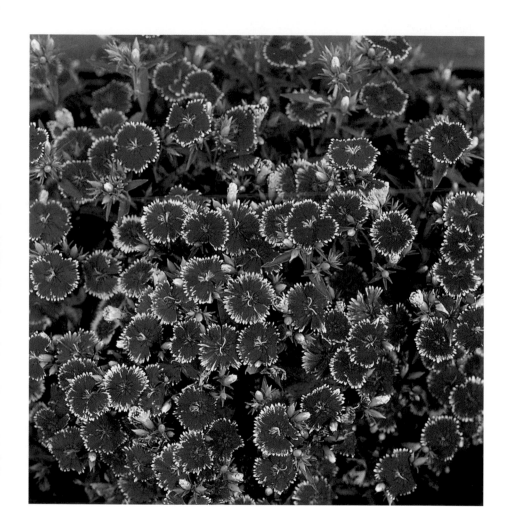

marguerite carnations that are used for bedding or borders. The fragrant flowers come in a wide color range and are borne atop long, branching stems.

GROWING NOTES

Sweet William and pinks do best in cool areas; they will grow in warm zones but not the tropics. Grow them in a sunny, warm spot, in well-drained, slightly alkaline soil. Dead-head frequently to prolong flowering. Avoid overwatering, for they dislike soggy soil. If biennial Sweet William are dead-headed immediately after flowering, they may overwinter and bloom again in early summer the following year. Carnations do best in cool temperatures, disliking hot and dry or wet summers. They need fertile, moist, and very well-drained soil. They may need support and can be propagated from softwood cuttings as well as from seed.

Opposite: A bicolored Sweet William.

Left: The bright flower colors and compact habit of Chinese or Indian pinks make them useful for edging paths or garden beds. The cultivar 'Regal Rose' is shown here.

DIASCIA HYBRIDS & CULTIVARS
TWINSPUR

These summer-flowering annuals and semi-evergreen perennials from South Africa have become widely known only in recent years. The flowers are small but massed in terminal racemes, generally shell pink, with more recent cultivars adding other soft shades of pink, mauve, salmon, and apricot to the genus, which gets its common name from the two short nectar spurs at the back of the flowers. These plants are low, mounded or trailing in habit, growing 10–12 in (25–30 cm) tall, and are suited to rock gardens, edging, containers, and hanging baskets.

Diascias are traditionally shell or rose pink, but modern breeding is extending the color range of these plants.

GROWING NOTES

Diascia grow best in temperate areas with mild winters, where they may grow for a few years, but they dislike extreme heat or high humidity. Elsewhere they may be grown as annuals; seed can be sown in the fall or spring for plants to flower 3–4 months later. These plants do best in full sun or light shade, in moist but well-drained soil, with regular watering. Remove spent blooms or cut back plants after the first flower flush to encourage another show.

DIERAMA PULCHERRIMUM
FAIRY FISHING ROD

Evoking visions of fairies at the bottom of the garden with their arched "fishing rods," these graceful plants, laden with pink tassels of tubular bells, add a touch of whimsy. *D. pulcherrimum* flowers primarily in shades of soft rose and carmine pink, but other cultivars bloom in white, red, and violet. With reed-like leaves shorter than the flowering stems, these plants suit being planted near a pond or water feature, especially if the area is moist. Blooms appear during spring, summer or fall, depending on the species and location. Fairy fishing rods grow to 5 ft (150 cm); allow room for these plants to spread. Dwarf forms include *D. dracomontanum*.

GROWING NOTES

Some varieties are tolerant of mild frost but are best suited to cool, warm temperate and frost-free locations. Grow these plants in full sun to partial shade, in well-drained soil kept moist during the growing season. Plant corms 3–5 in (8–13 cm) deep and at least 12 in (30 cm) apart, after the last spring or fall frosts. *Dierama* dislikes root disturbance.

Moist but well-drained soil is the key to keeping these plants thriving. Other common names for *D. pulcherrimum* are angel's fishing rod, fairy wand and wandflower.

HABRANTHUS SPECIES
RAIN LILY

They may look like look crocus, but these small showy bulbs are related to the *Hippeastrum* and *Zephyranthes* families. Originating in temperate South America, and not grown often enough, the mainly soft pink blooms brighten up rock gardens, borders, and containers, often appearing after summer or early fall rains—or a good watering. Best located through bulb specialists, the most commonly cultivated are *H. robustus* (syn. *Zephyranthes robusta*), sometimes known as pink rain lily, and *H. brachyandrus*, with its lavender-pink blooms and red center. Flowering with coppery-colored petals is *H. tubispathus*, while *H. martinezii* blooms in a cream shade.

H. robustus are best suited to warm, frost-free gardens, where they'll delight gardeners with their soft blooms, often appearing after rain—hence their common name.

GROWING NOTES
Not frost-hardy, these bulbs are best suited to tropical, subtropical, and frost-free gardens. In cooler climates, grow rain lily in a greenhouse before bringing it indoors to enjoy the blooms. Plant the bulbs in early fall, 2 in (5 cm) deep and 2–4 in (5–10 cm) apart, in free-draining, moisture-retentive soil. Keep the plants moist during the growing period and allow them to dry out during dormancy.

IBERIS UMBELLATA & I. AMARA
CANDYTUFT

Candytuft forms low, mounded plants growing to about 6–16 in (15–40 cm), making them useful for edging, bedding, borders, window boxes, and containers. Pure white forms are commonly included in a white garden, but the various strains of I. umbellata have umbrella-like, flattish heads of flowers in many shades of both light and bright pink, red-pink, and also mauve and purple. The taller growing I. amara has domed clusters of scented white or purplish white flowers. The large-flowered hyacinth forms have elongated spikes of flowers for a long season.

Iberis umbellata has an abundance of small, scented flowers.

GROWING NOTES
Candytuft will grow in most climates as long as it is in a warm, sunny spot. As it dislikes transplanting, sow it where it is to grow, in the fall or spring in cooler climates, in very well-drained, limey soil that need only be moderately fertile. Water to establish, then keep the soil on the dry side, for candytuft will not tolerate waterlogging. Monthly liquid feeds and light trimming after flushes will encourage strong flowering.

LAVATERA TRIMESTRIS
ROSE MALLOW

This is an annual that makes a statement! The annual mallow is an erect, branching, shrubby plant from the Mediterranean that bears silky, funnel shaped, dark pink, rose pink or brilliant white flowers 3 in (8 cm) across. Well-known cultivars include the prize-winning 'Silver Cup' and 'Mont Blanc'. Plants grow up to 32 in (80 cm) high or more, and spread to 18 in (45 cm), so they need lots of space. They have lobed, maple-like leaves, and while the flowers are short lived, they are borne in profusion. They can be grown as single specimens in gardens or containers, or used as background planting in an annual or mixed border.

Above: *Lavatera* 'Silver Cup' has bright rose pink flowers with dark veins.

Opposite: A tall grower, it is a useful back-of-the-border plant.

GROWING NOTES
Rose mallow will grow in most climates and soils, as long as it is in full sun in well-drained soil. Overly rich soil will encourage leaf growth at the expense of flowers. Water deeply each week. Sow seed where it is to grow in the fall in warm areas, in spring in cooler zones, or under glass in cold climate areas. These plants will self-sow.

NERINE SPECIES
GUERNSEY LILY

Guernsey lily or *Nerine sarniensis* is derived from 'Sarnia', the name given to the island of Guernsey by the Romans. It is said to be the first cultivated nerine in Europe. Originating in South Africa, these curved-petaled beauties with long stamens appear on naked stems during various stages of the fall, depending on the species or variety. The leaves flourish later, as late as spring with some varieties. Pink colors generally dominate the 30 or so species, with the shocking pink *N. bowdenii* being the most cultivated and cold tolerant; *N. undulata* has pink-fringed petals. Other species bloom in red (*N. sarniensis* and *N. fothergillii*) or white (*N. flexuosa* 'Alba'). With today's hybridizing techniques, various new forms and shades are on the market.

A simply stunning sight when planted en masse, nerines thrive in cool to subtropical climates.

GROWING NOTES

Nerines prefer cool to subtropical climates. Plant the bulb neck just above soil level, 4–6 in (10–15 cm) apart, in a sunny, sheltered location in spring or fall, depending on the variety. Mulch in cold areas or grow in greenhouses, bringing them indoors just before they flower. Nerines are good container plants.

PHLOX DRUMMONDII
PHLOX

Most strains of annual phlox come in mixed colors, with many shades of pink dominating.

The word *phlox* is Greek for "flame," which vividly describes the vibrant color of many *Phlox* species. While the dominant color of annual phlox is pink, including many shades of that color, they also come in reds, orange-reds, purples, mauves, and creams, often with a white or contrasting eye. Fast-growing to a bushy plant 6–12 in (15–30 cm) high, and long-flowering from spring or early summer to fall, phlox are usually planted in a mixed color range. They look their best in a massed display, but low-growers are good for edging and containers.

GROWING NOTES

Phlox grow in most climates in moderately rich, moist, well-drained soil. Give them plenty of water in the growing season, and add organic matter and mulch to help retain the moisture they need, but don't allow the soil to become soggy. Full sun is a requirement, and regular liquid feeding a beneficial extra. Sow seed *in situ* in early spring, or later in cooler areas.

RHODOHYPOXIS BAURII
ROSE GRASS

These floriferous little bloomers put on a mass display for long periods from spring to summer. Small clusters of dainty flowers, along with hairy leaves, appear on each stem. Reaching around 4–6 in (10–15 cm), these dwarf plants are ideal for a prize spot in the front of a border, rock or alpine garden, in a greenhouse, and in troughs and pots. For the best effect, plant *Rhodohypoxis baurii* en masse in single or mixed colors of blush pink, magenta or white. Many *Rhodohypoxis* hybrids—including the pink 'Margaret Rose', white 'Picta', and deep pink 'Albrighton'—are available.

Suitable for garden borders or containers, rose grass can be planted in a white or pink color scheme. For a dramatic touch, add bold purples.

GROWING NOTES

Best suited to cool and temperate gardens, rose grass is endemic to the wetland areas of the South African Drakensberg Mountains, which receive winter and spring snowfalls with temperatures to around 14°F (–10°C); the summers are cool and wet. Plant corms in well-drained, lime-free, moisture-retentive soil, in full sun. Add sharp sand for good drainage if required, and keep the soil relatively dry during the plants' dormant winter period. In frost-prone areas, apply mulch.

WATSONIA SPECIES
BUGLE LILY

Related to the iris, gladiolus, and freesia, the tall, majestic spikes of *Watsonia* create colorful, fragrant accents within a spring or summer garden border. One of the larger, commonly cultivated species is *W. borbonica* syn. *W. pyramidata*, in various shades of pink; the white form may be listed as *W. borbonica* subsp. *ardernei*. Allow space for these grow to 4–5 ft (1.2–1.5 m) in height. Better suited to pot culture are the dwarf species, such as *W. spectabilis*, *W. meriana* or *W. marginata*, which is also available as a taller form. With around 60 species and many cultivars, bugle lilies are often of mixed origin.

If space is limited, choose dwarf varieties, or grow bugle lily in large pots for a tall, contained display.

GROWING NOTES
The ideal growing conditions for these South African native plants are in subtropical, frost-free, and near frost-free gardens, although many named cultivars are hardy to 23°F (−5°C). Plant the corms in a sunny position in well-drained soil, 4–6 in (10–15 cm) deep. In colder climates, lift the bulbs in the fall, then leave them to dry before storing and replanting them in spring. In warm locations, plants may be regarded as environmental weeds.

WHITE

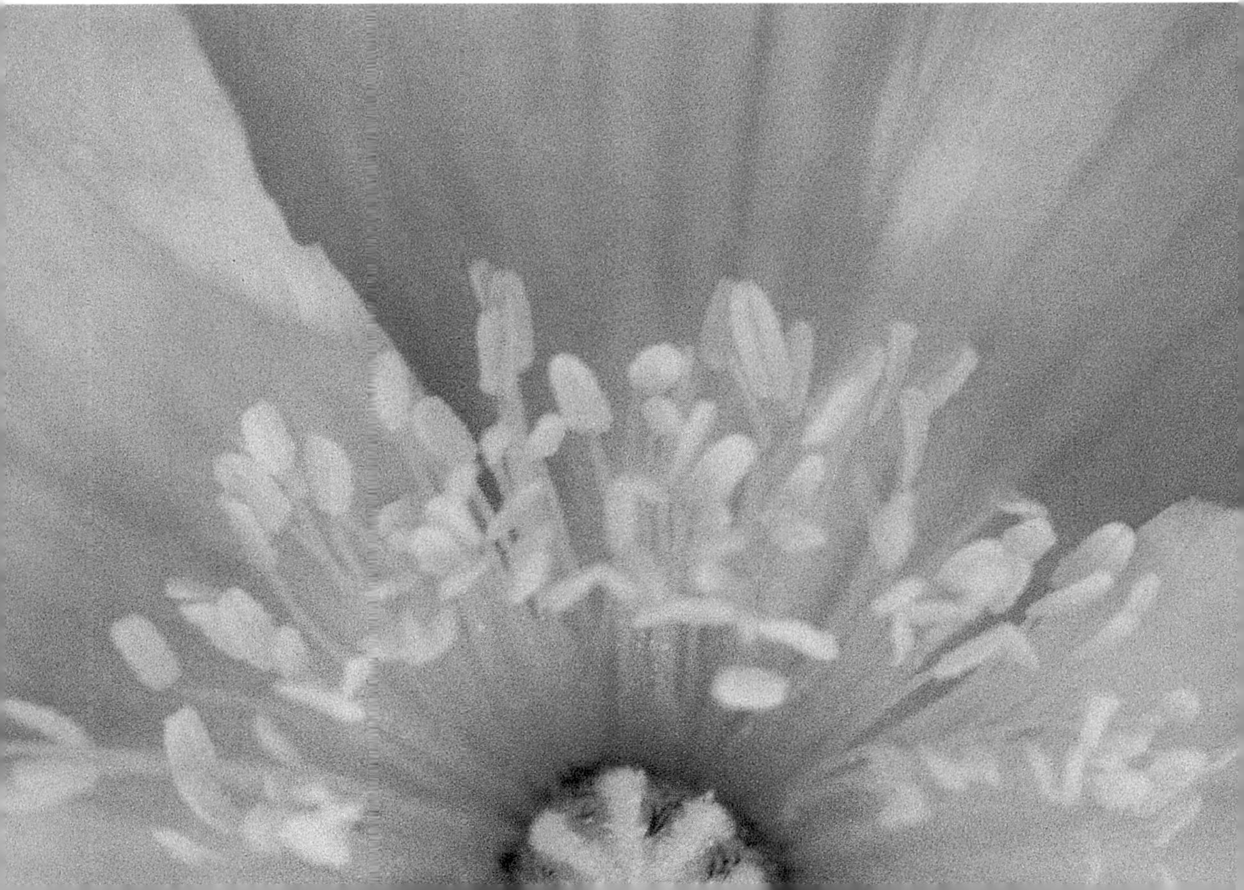

White is fresh and simple. It's the quintessential theme for weddings, name day celebrations, and remembrance, reflecting love, purity, and new beginnings. White befriends every other color—crisp and sharp against dark blue, indigo, and green; soft and beguiling with pastels. White brings a glow to shade, and reflects light at night or in moonlight.

Regardless of whether white is a true color or not, it's a timeless favorite, providing simplicity and classical elegance. For a serene effect, choose all-white flowers and plant these against a single-color backdrop of dark green or maroon foliage. Use white borders to enclose bolder colors or highlight areas near the house at night-time. Plant scented white flowers near windows.

White is one of the most versatile colors to use in any garden. Light and airy, white creates a frothy, frivolous effect; mass planted, it provides seamless continuity. Many annuals and bulbs detailed in "Multicolors" or "Pastel" will have pure white varieties too, or you can choose those that are predominantly white but have a touch of color for simple highlights.

CHRYSANTHEMUM PALUDOSUM SYN. LEUCANTHEMUM PALUDOSUM

SNOW DAISY

Known by several botanical names, these distinctive small daisy flowers with their dazzling white petals and yellow centers give rise to common and cultivar names that are variations on the theme of "snow daisy" and "snowland." Low-growing to 10–12 in (25–30 cm), with a similar spread, snow daisy is useful for edging, rock gardens, ground cover, and containers. Snow daisy flowers very quickly after planting and for a long period from spring through to fall, or in winter in hot climates. Not dissimilar in appearance is *Tanacetum parthenium* (syn. *Chrysanthemum parthenium*), the aromatic wildflower cultivated as the medicinal herb and known as feverfew. Although it is a perennial, feverfew is short lived, and is often grown as an annual.

Above: The medicinal herb feverfew, *Tanacetum parthenium*, can be grown as an annual and looks similar to the snow daisy.

Opposite: These small daisies have dazzling white petals and yellow disc centers.

GROWING NOTES

Easy to grow and relatively drought-tolerant, this annual prefers full sun but will tolerate a little shade. Sow *in situ* any time in warm zones; in cold climates wait until the soil warms up, or start indoors. Light, well-drained soil is all it needs. Snow daisy self-sows so freely that that it may become invasive.

CONVALLARIA MAJALIS
LILY-OF-THE-VALLEY

Lily-of-the-valley is a timeless, old-fashioned garden favorite whose fragrance is evoked in perfumes, soaps, and aromatic oils. But the best place to enjoy it is in the garden. With delicate, white, pearl-like flowers hanging from slightly arched stems during spring, and wide, slightly furled leaves, this plant is a delightful garden addition. Grow it in woodland-style gardens, in shady borders, as a ground cover or as a container plant to be "forced" for an indoor display. The flowers are normally single, but occasionally double-flowered plants are available. There's a rare pink form, sometimes labeled as 'Rosea', plus variegated-leaved varieties. Although its sweet red berries are used in homeopathic remedies, they are poisonous if ingested.

GROWING NOTES

Extremely cold-tolerant and frost-hardy, lily-of-the-valley is suited to cold and cool climates. Plant it in partial to total shade in fertile, moisture-retentive soil with good drainage. It will spread freely from rhizomes (or "pips"), planted 2 in (5 cm) deep and 2–3 in (5–8 cm) apart in the fall. Contain in pots for displays or to avoid an unwanted spread in the garden.

Opposite: Fragrant, pearl-like flowers adorn this cool-climate bulb.

Above: Grow lily-of-the-valley in shady borders, as a ground cover, or as a container plant to be "forced" for indoor display.

EUPHORBIA MARGINATA
SNOW-IN-SUMMER

The white markings of
Euphorbia marginata give
rise to common names
such as snow on the
mountain and ghost weed.

This relative of poinsettia is a bushy annual that grows up to 3 ft (1 m) high. The flowers, borne in terminal clusters, are not its main feature. Rather, it is the combination of oval gray-green leaves with white veins and margins, and the petal-like bracts around the flowers that are greenish white, margined, spotted or variegated that together give the impression of a coating of snow and ice. As a back-of-the-border plant it makes a good foil for brighter flowers, and adds coolness to the garden over a long summer-flowering period.

GROWING NOTES

This *Euphorbia* tolerates most climates and will endure cold conditions, but it does need a reasonable summer warmth to fully develop its white edging. Grow it in sun and light, well-drained soil from seed sown *in situ* in spring. Water it regularly while it is growing, but avoid overwatering, as this will cause the plants to rot. The poisonous milky sap can cause irritation.

GALANTHUS SPECIES & HYBRIDS
SNOWDROP

Often pushing up through blankets of snow to bloom, snowdrop is one of the northern hemisphere forerunners of spring. Unlike snowflake (*Leucojum* sp.), its exquisite white flowers have three shorter petals, adorned with small emerald green markings; the longer petals are usually pure white. Bulb specialists offer many species and hybrids, also flowering during fall and winter. The common snowdrop, *G. nivalis*, has many forms, including the double-flowered 'Flore Pleno' and 'Viridapicis', with green markings on all its petals. Tall-growing *G. elwesii* has flared flowers, while *G. reginae-olgae* blooms during fall.

GROWING NOTES
Most, but not all, species are hardy to 5°F (–15°C) or colder. Plant species suitable for your location as soon as they become available during fall. Snowdrops need moist, well-drained soil, preferably of neutral to slightly alkaline pH, shade or filtered light, and cool days. Divide immediately after flowering while the leaves are still green or when the bulbs are dormant. Apply mulch during summer.

Opposite: *Galanthus plicatus*, with its pleated, dark green leaves.

Above: Grow snowdrops in rock gardens, in drifts under deciduous trees, along woodland paths, and in containers.

GYPSOPHILA SPECIES
BABY'S BREATH

The airy cloud of tiny white or pink flowers and fine foliage of baby's breath makes it a very popular florist's flower, commonly used as a filler or foil to bolder flowers. It can create a similar effect in the garden, where it could be planted more often, in drifts in borders and rock gardens, or planted beneath roses. *G. elegans* is a true annual; the numerous named varieties generally have single flowers. The often double florist's flower is usually the perennial *G. paniculata*, but it is mostly grown as an annual in gardens. *G. muralis* is a dwarf-growing, pink-flowered European native, suitable for edging, containers, and hanging baskets.

Useful as a cut flower, baby's breath can seem like a lovely floating cloud in the garden.

GROWING NOTES

Baby's breath does best in cool climates, but it will grow in all but tropical zones. It needs full sun and shelter from strong wind, and well-drained, slightly alkaline soil. Additional organic matter aids growth, but baby's breath is moderately drought tolerant, so once it is established a deep, weekly watering will suffice. Sow seeds *in situ* in the fall or spring. The flowering season is short; sow fortnightly in spring for a continuous supply of blooms.

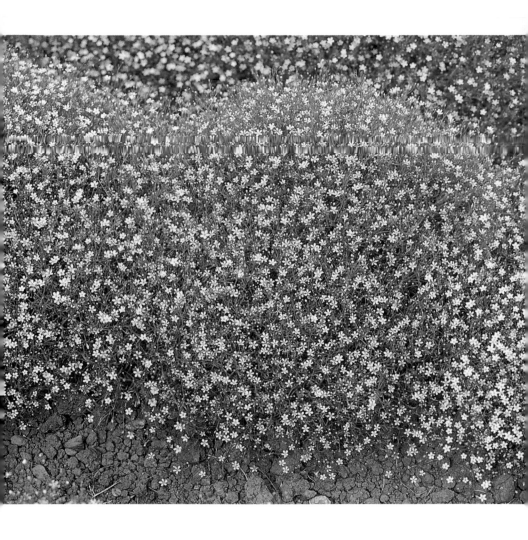

HYMENOCALLIS SPECIES
SPIDER LILY

With flowers displaying a large corona, projected stamens, and long, slender petals, these striking plants put on an extended summer show. Their bulbs produce large clumps of strappy leaves with fragrant, normally white flowers on stout stems. Deciduous or evergreen, depending on climate and species, the foliage may look a little untidy during dormancy. In cooler locations, grow these plants indoors. Commonly grown species include the marginally frost-hardy *H.* x *festalis*, the tropical *H. littoralis* and *H. narcissiflora*, and the dramatic yellow cultivar *H.* 'Sulphur Queen'. A variegated hybrid is also available.

GROWING NOTES
Hymenocallis are native to areas of tropical America, Peru, Africa, the West Indies, and the United States. Various species can be grown in tropical through to near frost-free locations. Some may need mulching or overwintering in a frost-free spot in cool or winter-wet zones. Grow in full sun or light shade, with protection from strong winds, in humus-rich, well-drained soil. Allow plenty of space for growth.

Opposite: Apt common names, such as Peruvian daffodil, reflect various species's daffodil- or lily-like appearance; the colors may also be ivory and yellow. *H.* x *festalis* is shown here.

Above: An evergreen species of spider lily.

IPOMOEA ALBA SYN. *CALONYCTION ACULEATUM*
MOONFLOWER

By the light of the silvery moon...deliciously fragrant moonflowers open at sunset and take on a silvery sheen by moonlight.

There are a number of *Ipomoea* species or morning glories that are twining, climbing annuals, but since some can become extremely invasive, especially in warm and tropical climates, they are not generally recommended. Care should be taken in selecting species and preventing them from becoming a weedy garden escapee. But we couldn't resist including *I. alba* for the loveliness of its large, satiny, creamy white flowers that open on summer nights to fill the air with their delicious fragrance. Originating in South America, these vines are rampantly perennial in hot climates, where they will grow more than 15 ft (5 m), but they can be grown as an annual wherever there are warm summers.

GROWING NOTES

Obviously moonflower is easiest to grow in warm climates. Growing it in a tub will help restrict its height, and may also enable you to grow it on a sunny patio in cooler locations. It will need wire or a trellis on which to climb. Moonflower is hard to grow in greenhouses.

LEUCOJUM SPECIES & HYBRIDS
SNOWFLAKE

Taller growing than snowdrops (*Galanthus* sp.) and more suited to warmer climates, you can tell these dainty little plants apart by their equal-sized white petals with small green or yellow spots at the tips. Flowering times and heights vary between the many species: in the northern hemisphere, *L. vernum* is known as the spring snowflake, with stems 8 in (20 cm) long; growing taller to 2 ft (60 cm) is *L. aestivum*, called the summer snowflake (flowering late winter to spring in the southern hemisphere), with a popular, large-bloomed, robust cultivar called 'Gravetye Giant'. Finally, only 5 in (12 cm) tall is the fall snowflake, *L. fallale*. Flowering mid- to late-season is the wrare, pink-flushed *L. roseum*.

Opposite: *Leucojum aestivum*, or snowflakes, are taller growing than snowdrops, and more suitable for warmer climes.

GROWING NOTES

Grow snowflake in locations ranging from cold to warm temperate; it is not suited to subtropical or warmer climates. Plant fall-flowering species in mid to late summer, and spring- and early summer-flowerers in the fall in a sunny or partially shaded position. Plant snowflake 3–4 in (8–10 cm) deep and 4–8 in (10–20 cm) apart in moist, well-drained soil, preferably with a neutral to slightly alkaline pH.

Above: Divide snowflake every 3–4 years, after the foliage has died down.

ORNITHOGALUM THYRSOIDES
CHINCHERINCHEE

Chincherinchee are the ultimate cut flowers or container plants.

Starting at the base of each pyramid-shaped cluster, starry petals gradually open and put on a striking show for many weeks during summer. Chincherinchee grows to about 1 ft (30 cm) tall with white, almost green-white flowers. Other popular species have varying geographic origins, flower in spring or fall, and can be cold tolerant. Some naturalize well but may be invasive. Colorful cultivars, although not widely available, have more open flowers of bright yellow and orange, and are labelled 'Chesapeake' hybrids.

GROWING NOTES

O. thyrsoides originated in South Africa and is best suited to frost-free, cool temperate to subtropical climates. Plant bulbs 2 in (5 cm) deep and space them 4–6 in (10–15 cm) apart during spring in moist, well-drained soil, in full sun or partial shade. Increase the amount of water as flowering begins. In frost-prone climates, dig up bulbs and store in the fall; reduce or withhold watering during the dormant period. Divide clumps every 2–3 years. Grow in pots as indoor displays or greenhouse plants if your climate doesn't allow for garden cultivation; keep the pots in cool temperatures.

ZEPHYRANTHES CANDIDA
RAIN FLOWER

From tropical America and the West Indies, these delightful crocus-like flowers are apt to suddenly bloom after rain in late summer or fall. Easy to grow, *Zephyranthes candida* can be grown as a specimen clump, but are best planted en masse to show off the stunning pure white petals and prominent yellow stamens. This plant grows to 8 in (20 cm) tall, with narrow leaves resembling those of onions. Within the genus there are many species (and a couple of hybrids) that bloom in shades of yellow or pink. As botanic classifications change, some species are still labelled *Habranthus*.

GROWING NOTES
Mildly frost-tolerant, these bulbs are best suited to frost-free temperate, subtropical, and tropical gardens. Grow autumn crocus in dappled shade (in warm climates), otherwise in full sun; in frost-prone locations, grow it in a greenhouse and bring it indoors to enjoy the blooms. Plant bulbs from spring until summer, 2 in (5 cm) deep and 2–4 in (5–10 cm) apart, in free-draining, moisture-retentive soil. Keep moist during the growing period, and allow the bulbs to dry out during dormancy.

Opposite: As these plants are apt to suddenly bloom after rain in late summer or fall, they are often known by the common names autumn crocus and storm lily.

Above: *Zephyranthes candida* and portulaca.

Timeless and enduring, pastels are the soft hues of red, pink, blue, yellow, and white. They're gentle rose pink, baby blue, cream, and lime green. Pastels create a calm, gentle mood, quietening the senses. These are touches of color that speak softly, whisper alluringly. Use these delicate shades where bolder tones are too loud or where white is too stark.

For the best effects, use pale powder blues, soft pinks, and creams in areas receiving first light or fading daylight. Pastels are romantic and soft as well as versatile companions. Plant en masse with highlights of stronger colors for balance and effect. Create pockets of pastels to subdue bolder colors. Blend white with stronger colors, then add pastels to link them both.

Plant pastels for a whisper, not a shout. Discreet in color, pastels can suit any garden style, whether fused with more distinctive tones or planted alone. Use pastels to lift shady, dull areas, and to bring out a soft glow or add gentle color against white walls. For other choices, look in the "Multicolors" section, as well as in the specific color chapters.

AQUILEGIA X HYBRIDA
COLUMBINE

Although generally classified as a hardy herbaceous perennial, columbine or granny's bonnets has been included for those gardeners in temperate regions who need to start them at least every second year if they are lucky, annually if they aren't so lucky. In warmer climates it's probably best to buy them as potted plants, and you will, if only because you'll find them irresistible. They have dainty, gray-green, maidenhair-like foliage, and the charming long-spurred flowers on tall thin stems, 16–28 in (40–70 cm) tall, come in a wide range of solid pastel colors and bicolors. Columbines are essential in a cottage garden, lovely in any garden, and wonderful as cut flowers.

GROWING NOTES
Aquilegias are not suited for either the tropics or hot, dry areas. In cooler climates you can sow seed in the fall or spring, in pots or directly into the garden, and they may self-seed. Grow them in full sun in cool areas, but in warm areas they prefer partial shade with some morning sun. Columbines need compost-enriched soil and regular, deep watering so that they don't dry out.

Above: Although perennial in cold climates, columbines are best treated as annuals in temperate areas.

Opposite: Aquilegias come in a large range of pastel colors and combinations.

CLEOME HASSLERIANA SYN. C. SPINOSA
SPIDER FLOWER

It is sometimes surprising that these unusual and curious plants work so well in the garden. The spider-like appearance comes from the long stamens and styles that protrude from the narrow-petaled flowers. The flowers—in shades of pink, rose, mauve, and white—sit atop single, upright, 4–5 ft (1.2–1.5 m), hairy and spiny stems with lance-shaped leaflets. With their soft, subdued colors and airy flower heads, spider flowers make interesting background plantings or attractive feature plantings. They grow rapidly and are long flowering, from summer through to fall, and they can be used as cut flowers. The scent of the flowers is most noticeable at night.

Spidery *Cleome* flowers—in shades of pink, rose, mauve, and white—sit on top of tall, erect stems.

GROWING NOTES
These are frost-tender plants from subtropical South America, so they thrive in a warm, sunny position and don't mind humidity. Sow seed in spring or early summer, or plant them when the danger of frost has passed. Spider flowers also enjoy well-drained, fertile soil, protection from strong winds, and regular watering. In cooler climates, they can be grown as conservatory plants.

Above: Foxgloves, growing here with Russell lupins, add height to a border.

Opposite: With their clusters of bell-shaped flowers, foxglove spires add drama to gardens in early summer.

DIGITALIS PURPUREA
FOXGLOVE

The various seedling strains and hybrids of foxgloves are grown as annuals, biennials or perennials, depending on the climate. The statuesque flower spires, which may reach 6 ft (2 m) tall, look best as background plants or mass planted informally in a woodland or cottage garden. The tubular, two-lipped flowers come in a range of soft colors from light pink to magenta and purple, plus white and cream, while some border on apricot-pink and creamy yellow, and many have heavily spotted throats. All parts of the plant are poisonous.

GROWING NOTES

As a biennial, foxgloves are sown in spring in the first year and grow through summer to the stage where their basal leaves form a rosette that overwinters, the flower spikes emerging the following spring. They won't overwinter in very cold climates, but can be grown as an annual. Members of the Foxy Group bloom readily in the first year from seed. They can be grown in sun in cool climates, but are best in dappled shade in rich, moist, well-drained soil.

EUCOMIS SPECIES
PINEAPPLE LILY

These star performers, crowned with pineapple-like leaves,
bloom in a mass of tiny flowers. Usually growing from
1 to 3 ft (30 cm to 1 m) and seeming almost top-heavy when in
full glory, pineapple lilies create a stunning display when
planted en masse in a sunny garden position. The star-shaped
flowers, borne in summer, can be combinations of green with
white, purple, bronze or pale yellow; the leaves may be purple.
Most widely available are the lightly scented *E. comosa* and the
popular yellow-green *E. fallalis*. *E. bicolor* is white-flowered,
bordered in purple; the giant *E. pallidiflora* is rarer and more
tender; and *E. zambesiaca* is a dwarf form.

Opposite: *Eucomis* are
excellent as long-lasting
cut flowers. *E. fallalis* is
shown here.

Above: *Eucomis comosa.*

GROWING NOTES
Marginally frost-tolerant, these deciduous bulbs are best suited
to warm temperate climates. In frost-prone areas, mulch well or
grow *Eucomis* as indoor potted plants. Plant so that the bulb
neck is just above ground level, in fertile, well-drained soil.
Water well during their growing season. Keep pineapple lilies
dry during the winter dormant period. These plants prefer full
sun but will tolerate some shade, particularly in hot climates.

EUSTOMA GRANDIFLORUM
SYN. *LISIANTHUS RUSSELLIANUS*

TEXAS BLUEBELL

Gorgeous...in the garden or in a vase, but not the easiest annual to grow.

Chances are you will get to know these gorgeous flowers in a floristry shop before you see them in a garden. They are native to the American prairies, where they have purplish cup-shaped flowers, but cultivated varieties, largely bred in Japan, have single or double flowers in pastel shades of purple, blue, pink, yellow, and white, often with picotee edging. Some say they resemble roses; others describe them as tulip- or poppy-like. They have become very popular as cut flowers due to their beauty and long vase life.

GROWING NOTES

These aren't plants for the beginner. They're even challenging for cut-flower growers. You will find them being offered by seed houses to be grown as annuals or biennials, but it's probably best to buy and grow them as potted plants. Plant them in deep pots, as they have a long tap root, and enjoy them as a living bunch of flowers that your friends will envy. Place them on a sunny patio or in a light, airy conservatory in perfectly drained, neutral to alkaline soil.

Above: The clusters of small four-petaled flowers almost completely hide the gray-green foliage.

Opposite: Commonly white, Sweet Alice also comes in shades of pink and lilac, often two-toned with white.

LOBULARIA MARITIMA
ALYSSUM

Once known as *Alyssum maritimum*, this fast-growing, low, spreading plant that grows about 4 in (10 cm) high and 8–12 in (20–30 cm) wide is an unpretentious but extremely useful annual. The rounded clusters of small, honey-scented flowers bloom for a long period, even all year round in warm climates. Commonly white, alyssum flowers also come in shades of lilac, violet, and pink. Alyssum is used for edging in garden beds and rock gardens, and as a filler in hanging baskets and window boxes, or any type of container.

GROWING NOTES
Alyssum grows in most climates other than the tropics; wherever it grows, it needs full sun to perform at its best. Sweet Alice will flourish in light, well-drained soil, but will tolerate most other types as long as the drainage is good. It even tolerates dryness, so water it well while it is establishing, then let the soil dry out between waterings. Monthly liquid feeds and regular shearing back after flower flushes will encourage continuous blooming. Sow *in situ*, or plant any time to suit the climate. This plant will self-sow.

MALCOLMIA MARITIMA
VIRGINIAN STOCK

This is another modest but useful annual. Useful because it is fast growing, taking only 4–5 weeks from seed to flowering, and because it grows only to a compact 8–12 in (20–30 cm), making it handy for stop-gap planting and for filling in a border. It is also useful as an edging plant and in containers, and it combines well with spring-flowering bulbs. Most commonly mauve with a white eye, the fragrant flowers of Virginian stock also come in shades of pink, red, and white.

Virginian stock is a useful fast-growing dwarf annual that grows wild on sandy places near the sea in Greece and Albania.

GROWING NOTES

Virginian stock can be grown in warm to cool areas; it prefers full sun, but will tolerate some shade in hotter climates. The soil should be well drained and neutral to alkaline—so add lime if necessary—but it needn't be very rich. These plants don't transplant well, so sow seed *in situ* in the fall or spring. Successive sowing will prolong the flowering season, and the plants self-seed freely.

NICOTIANA SPECIES & HYBRIDS

FLOWERING TOBACCO

Nicotiana x sanderae
Domino Series 'Mixed'.

Ornamental tobacco plants should be admired, not smoked or eaten, for these plants are poisonous. But you can certainly sniff them, because the flowers are often fragrant, particularly at night. Several species and numerous cultivars of the garden hybrids *N.* x *sanderae* may overwinter in warm zones and microclimates, but they are commonly grown as annuals. Their flowers, unlike some *Nicotiana* blooms, are flat and upward-facing, and remain open in bright sunlight. They come in pastel tones of greenish yellow, salmon pink, rose pink, lime-purple, and other shades of pink, red, and purple. The flaring, long, tubular white blooms of *N. sylvestris* open only in the evening or on cloudy days. This tall plant requires plenty of space.

GROWING NOTES
Nicotiana flowers best in warm weather and should be grown in sun or dappled shade, although *N. sylvestris* needs denser shade. They are best grown where their night scent can be enjoyed in fertile, moist but well-drained soil. More compact cultivars look good in containers. The seeds need light to germinate so they must be surface-sown.

NIGELLA DAMASCENA
LOVE-IN-A-MIST

There are around 20 species of these annuals, most of them to be found growing along roadsides and in cornfields in southern Europe, western Asia, and North Africa. As pretty as its romantic common name, *N. damascena* is the best known garden species. With its elegant filigree foliage and spurred, many-petaled flowers, the aptly named love-in-a-mist has a soft, hazy appearance. It is grown for both its pretty flowers and decorative balloon-like seed pods that account for its other common name of devil-in-a-bush. The flower colors range from sky blue to deep violet-blue, plus pink and white. 'Miss Jekyl' is the best known double blue form. Love-in-a-mist looks at home in a cottage garden, but can also be mass planted or used as a filler in borders and between shrubs.

Opposite. The inflated seed pods are also attractive and can be dried.

Above: The pretty flowers and feathery foliage of love-in-a-mist make it lovely in the garden or as a cut flower.

GROWING NOTES

Love-in-a-mist will grow in most climates, preferring full sun to slight shade. It isn't fussy about soil quality, but requires good drainage. *N. damascena* dislikes being transplanted, so sow it *in situ* in the fall or spring in cooler areas, at intervals to extend the harvest. These plants self-seed with abandon.

EVENING PRIMROSE

E vening primroses have a number of things going for them. They have delicate cupped flowers, in gentle shades of shell pink, white, and lemon yellow. They also have fragrance, often only dispensed when the flowers open their petals at night, hence the common name. And some species, particularly *O. biennis*, have medicinal properties. Their disadvantage is that the most popular garden species and cultivars are somewhat invasive perennials, especially the pale pink forms of *O. speciosa*. There are a number of annual species or short-lived perennials that will flower in their first year, including the pink-flowered *O. kunthiana* and *O. rosea*, and the Missouri primrose, the yellow-flowering *O. macrocarpa* (syn. *O. missouriensis*).

Many species of evening primrose are popular ornamentals, with soft pink, night-scented flowers such as these.

GROWING NOTES

Evening primroses are adaptable plants that grow well in most warm to cool areas. The fact that they have become naturalized in many parts of the world is an indication that they can quite readily become garden thugs, for they spread from running roots as well as seedlings. They will thrive in full sun, but tolerate some shade and almost any sharp-draining soil, even tolerating dry conditions.

POLIANTHES TUBEROSA
TUBEROSE

Tuberoses are among the most fragrant of garden plants, grown for both the cut-flower industry and perfume production. Depending on the location, they may bloom in late summer, fall or even into winter. Their flowering spikes reach 2–4 ft (70–120 cm), with single creamy white flowers tinged with pink. Tuberose has long, slender, grass-like foliage.

GROWING NOTES

Native to Mexico—another common name is Mexican tuberose—tuberoses should be grown in cool to tropical areas in full sun, with shelter from strong winds, or in a heated greenhouse. They need well-drained soil, enriched with organic matter. Guidelines on planting techniques vary considerably between growers in different locations, so ask for local advice. Depending on the conditions, the tubers may be planted at soil level, or at a depth of 2 in (5 cm). You may be advised to dig the tubers up and store them over winter; or you may have better results leaving them *in situ* or treating them as annuals, replacing them each year. Plant tuberoses in late winter to early spring (after the last frosts).

Opposite: Another common name for *Polyanthes tuberosa* is polyanthus lily.

Above: Often more widely available is the semi-double form, 'The Pearl'.

PRIMULA MALACOIDES & P. OBCONICA

PRIMROSE

Primula malacoides is also known as fairy primrose.

Growing in the shady valleys and woods of western China, these primroses look delicate but are in fact surprisingly tough. The cultivated forms are more elegant than their multicolored *Polyanthus* cousin we met earlier (see page 128). They are similarly perennial in cooler climates, but are most often grown as annuals. Pale mauve in the wild, garden strains of *P. malacoides* have whorls of small, flat, single or double flowers in cool pink, mauve, purple, carmine, and white. They look best when planted in drifts and between shrubs or in a woodland setting; a clumped planting of pure white *P. malacoides* is particularly attractive.

Primroses flower from late winter to midspring in warm climates, later in cool climates, and also make excellent container plants. The pastel pinks, salmons, blues, and white of *P. obconica* make it a popular floristry line for indoor display. Frost-tender, it can also be grown as a pot plant in a conservatory, fernery or shade house, or grown in warm-climate gardens with winter sunlight. Contact with the foliage sometimes causes skin irritation; however, modern strains have been bred to be free of the chemical that causes it.

Opposite: A delightful drift of *Primula obconica* in a woodland setting.

Left: *P. obconica* comes in many pastel shades of pinks, salmons, blue, and white, and in deeper tones as well.

GROWING NOTES

P. malacoides can be grown in the garden in most climates. In warm zones it needs semishade, but in cool climates it will thrive in a frost-free, sunny spot. Plant it in early fall to late winter into organically-enriched soil that has good drainage, but keep it moist and liquid feed the plant when it is in flower. It self-seeds, but the following year's flowers will rarely be vigorous or come true, so it is better to plant afresh. *P. obconica* will do best in a frost-protected environment or indoors in a free-draining potting mix, placed in bright, filtered light.

THE EFFECTS OF CLIMATE

Wherever you live, whsatever annuals or bulbs you want to grow, the determining factor is the minimum temperature plants will be exposed to. Therefore they are grouped into "cold-climate" and "warm-climate" types, according to their natural origins. Many "cold-climate" plants occur in cold or cool parts of Europe, North America, and Asia where temperatures may drop to freezing or colder, producing frost or snow; others may originate in cool temperate and frost-free areas. "Warm-climate" plants originate in warm temperate (frost-free) and tropical areas in locations including South Africa, Mediterranean countries, West and Central Asia, and the Americas.

Depending on their frost-tolerance, plants are usually defined as hardy, half-hardy or tender, so in order to grow them successfully, select those most suitable for your location. Half-hardy and tender bulbs usually need to be dug up and stored over winter, while hardy bulbs can be left *in situ*.

Wet and dry seasons vary between continents, with summer rainfall and winter rainfall dictating plants' needs. If you live in a location with a reversed climate, some plants, especially bulbs, may be difficult, but not necessarily impossible, to grow. Other factors, such as length of growing season and humidity, can play their part too.

If you don't have optimum conditions, try creating microclimates to provide a more supportive environment. Plant or erect screens to provide shade or wind protection, site plants against a warm wall for shelter, install irrigation equipment to provide moisture, or construct a warm greenhouse to raise humidity and temperature levels.

And if you're determined to try and grow a plant not ideally suited to your climate zone, look at alternatives within its genus, as there may be natural species or cultivated varieties tolerant of conditions at the upper or lower limits of the "normal" range.

BUYING & CHOOSING ANNUALS

You can grow annuals from seed or seedlings you have bought, or from seed you have saved yourself. Starting from seed is cheaper; some plants perform better if grown this way, and there are a great many varieties available that you won't find as seedlings. Garden centers usually offer a basic range, but ordering by mail or the Internet will give you access to an enormous range. Enthusiasts enjoy poring over new season's catalogs for the unusual and the obscure; beginners may well appreciate the fact that seed companies often package collections of varieties that may be color coordinated or chosen because they flower at the same time—a boon if you aren't sure what to plant with what. Check the use-by date on the seed pack, for seed only remains fresh and viable for a set period.

Seedlings

On the other hand, many varieties of annuals are sold as seedlings or young plants, which is great if you don't want to bother with the seed-sowing stage or you want a head start. Seedlings are usually sold in trays or punnets, sometimes divided into cells, which results in stronger seedlings and minimizes transplant shock when you remove them, ready for planting. You can buy semi-advanced seedlings and more established plants in pots that can be transplanted to the garden or into containers. Buying seedlings or plants is more expensive, but the results are instant and easier to plan. Choose plants that have healthy foliage, good roots, and sturdy, compact growth. Avoid any that have become leggy, with drawn stems, or that have yellow, diseased or dead leaves, or are sitting in dried-out compost.

Growing from seed

Depending on the plant variety, the time of the year, when plants are to flower, and the climate, seed may be sown into trays or pots for transplanting as seedlings. Alternatively, seed may be sown *in situ*, or direct into the garden where they are to grow. This is best for plants with relatively large seed, for those that produce strong seedlings, or for plants that dislike root disturbance. Some seeds can be sown by either method, but some are small and delicate, and require too much shelter and attention for direct sowing. We have indicated some preferences in individual plant entries, but the information on seed packs, combined with your own knowledge of local climate and weather conditions, should be your final guide.

Sowing seed in trays or containers

You can sow seed into plastic seed trays, cell packs or various types of containers. Seed trays are usually quite adequate; even used margarine tubs or milk cartons will do, as long as you wash them thoroughly and punch some holes in them for drainage.

1 Fill the container with a very open, well-drained, fertilizer-free seed-raising mix. Level off the mix.

2 Using a presser, firm gently to about ½ in (1 cm) below the rim.

3 Sow seed thinly, aiming for even coverage.

4 Sow seed to a depth that is about equivalent to the seed's diameter. Cover with a layer of sieved compost. Very small seeds do not need to be covered.

5 Label, and water either by standing the tray in water or using a watering can with a fine rose. Place a sheet of clear plastic or glass over the tray to retain heat and moisture.

6 Cover with a sheet of newspaper or netting to protect the seeds from direct sunlight.

Depending on the climate and time of the year, place the tray in a sunny or shaded position outdoors, or indoors or in a heated frame or propagation unit. Remove the covers as germination begins.

Pricking out

In warm climates it may be possible to transplant seedlings direct from their containers into the garden bed or pot in which they are to grow. But in cooler climates they often go through a transition stage. As soon as seedlings in trays are large enough to handle (see the picture at left) they need to be transplanted, or pricked out, into larger containers so that they are grown on without becoming drawn and weak due to overcrowding.

Have a tray, pot or cells with planting holes ready, filled with potting mix, and using a pencil, planting stick or dibber, gently prise out and separate the seedlings. Handling them only by their seed leaves, lower them gently into a hole so that the seed leaves are just above soil level. Very small seeds such as those of alyssum and lobelia can be transplanted in small clumps. Using the dibber, firm the soil around them. Label, then water them using a fine spray and place them in a frame, greenhouse or warm, shaded spot until the seedlings are 3–4 in (8–10 cm) tall and ready for planting.

Tender annuals raised in controlled conditions must be gradually hardened off or acclimatized to outdoor growing conditions before being planted out. Damping off is a fungal disease that causes seeds or seedlings to rot. It occurs especially in humid weather or if seedlings are overcrowded and overwatered. Prevention is better than cure. Avoid sowing too thickly, and overwatering or watering in the evening. Keep the seed trays well ventilated. Only use a fungicide if absolutely necessary.

Direct sowing

Seed can be sown direct into a garden bed, but some sound preparation will result in a better display. Here is a basic preparation method. While most annuals like a moderately rich, friable, well-drained soil that is slightly alkaline, some have different requirements, such as less fertile soil or additional lime, so adjust the mix according to the particular species and the instructions on the seed packet.

1 Dig over the bed, and remove weeds.

2 Add in some well-rotted organic matter, such as compost or animal manure, and a small quantity of complete fertilizer. Rake in some lime if necessary.

3 Rake, level, and firm the soil to achieve a fine, loose, crumbly surface.

4 Sow seed in drills for straight, regular rows, or broadcast or scatter them for a more informal, natural look.

5 You could mark out irregular-shaped patches for different annuals.

6 Cover with a sprinkling of sieved soil or seed-raising mix to the right depth. Gently tamp them down and water thoroughly with a fine spray.

Sow seed as thinly and evenly as possible to avoid seedlings being spindly. Thin them out as they germinate if necessary. Later thinnings may be transplanted. Water, weed, protect them from slugs and snails, and tend them regularly until they germinate and the young seedlings are growing strongly. Planting distances between annuals vary according to the type of plant and the size to which they will grow. We haven't provided universal rules in this book, as seed packets or seedling labels will provide the appropriate distance for each plant.

Planting seedlings

Whether you have purchased seedlings or grown them from seed, plant them out on a cool day, or in the cool of the morning or evening. Water the punnets or pots an hour or so before removing the seedlings.

1 Dig planting holes large enough to accommodate the roots comfortably in a bed or border or prepared containers (see page 440).

2 Remove the plants carefully. In a cell punnet, you can squeeze the bottom of each cell; in a tray, gently prise plants apart, taking care not to damage the roots and to keep as much soil around them as possible.

3 Plant seedlings at the depth they were in the container. Backfill the hole and firm the soil gently around the roots.

4 Water with a fine spray, and sprinkle snail bait, as snails and slugs just love young seedlings. Mulch around seedlings to retain moisture in the soil.

Placing some water-absorbing crystals around the roots is a good idea in hot, dry districts. Watering in seedlings with a seaweed solution will help give them a good start in life, and this can be repeated fortnightly. Position stakes or twiggy supports for tall growers at this stage so you won't damage their roots later on.

Maintaining & growing annuals

Once established, most annuals are very easy to grow. Keep them well watered while they are establishing, then water them less often but thoroughly to encourage a deep root system. A good layer of mulch around the plants will help prevent the soil from drying out. Pinching out the growing tips of some young plants encourages them to branch and makes a bushier plant with more flowers, but don't do this with some annuals, such as delphiniums and bachelor's buttons. Regular liquid feeding with a water-soluble fertilizer helps most plants to bloom for a longer period, and regular weeding is a must, as weeds compete for nutrients and water. The more regularly you pick blooms or remove spent flowers, the more you will encourage fresh flowering, for once annuals set seed they complete their life cycle. Tie tall growers to stakes or supports as they grow.

Saving seed

If you want to save seed from plants you must allow the flowers to die naturally on the plant. Use strong, healthy plants. Let the seed pod or capsule dry thoroughly on the plant, then shake the seeds into a paper bag. Alternatively, cut off the seed heads just before they split and spread them on a newspaper-lined tray, then place the tray in a warm, sunny, well-ventilated spot. When the seed head or capsule is dry, shake out the seeds, discarding any that have been damaged. Store seed in a labeled envelope in a cool, dry place until sowing time. Note that the saved seed may not produce a plant identical to its parent and many may be inferior. This is especially true of named hybrid plants.

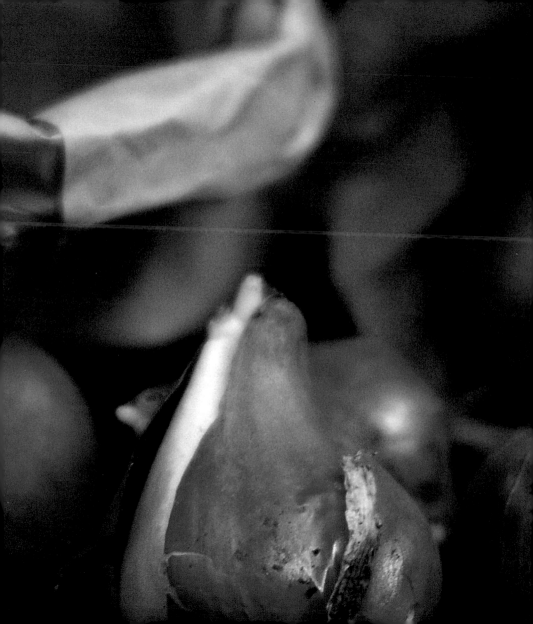

BUYING BULBS

How do you choose bulbs from the mouth-watering array becoming more widely available and more diverse? Local nurseries tend to carry a basic range, perfect for the novice. But if you want to experiment further, seek out specialist growers or associations, and browse mail order and Internet catalogs. Always check the planting times recommended for your location to ensure your order is timed correctly.

Many suppliers offer "mixed" bulbs that may be a collection of different types of bulbs, or mixed colors of the one type. Bulbs such as daffodils and tulips are often graded and priced according to size. Purchase the best bulbs you can afford—the larger the better. Buy bulbs with staggered flowering times; choose early-, mid- and late-flowering varieties for an ongoing display. And don't just stick to the same old favorites. Why not order a couple you're unfamiliar with?

Discard or avoid buying bulbs that are damaged or withered, or display signs of mold or rot. Plant bulbs immediately, especially any with small, new shoots emerging. Those not showing growth can be stored in mesh or paper bags in a cool, dry place if it's not possible to plant them out. Supermarkets and chainstores will often display bulbs with obvious growth long past their prime. Avoid buying these. Also most of these outlets don't employ horticulturists to give advice. For the best results, stick to buying bulbs from the experts.

Bulb types

The term "bulb" is applied to a range of plants with some type of underground (or near the surface) storage organ that will sustain the plant through its dormant period of either a cold winter or a hot, dry summer.

True bulbs have fleshy scales or modified leaves that are loose and open (such as liliums), or compact (such as hyacinths); they may also be covered by a thin, papery "tunic." At their base is a small, modified stem, called a basal plate, from which roots emerge and new bulbs, called "offsets" or "bulblets," are produced. In some cases the parent bulb dies, leaving the bulblets. A few plants, like lilies, form bulblets on the stem or in the leaf axis.

Corms are modified, thickened, fleshy stems with thin, scaly leaves. The parent plant is replaced each year by a growing point or "eye" on the top that forms a new plant. Some also produce "cormels" or small corms that grow from around the basal plate of the parent plant; these may take several years to flower.

Rhizomes are horizontal, underground stems without a basal plate but with growth buds along the top and roots along the bottom. To propagate plants such as iris, dig up and divide each clump into smaller plants by cutting the rhizome into sections of at least 3 in (8 cm), retaining a new bud and roots on each.

Tubers are similar to rhizomes, but are swollen and fleshier, with scattered "eyes" or buds that are used for propagation.

1 Grape hyacinth (bulb). 2 Ranunculus (corm). 3 Cape Cowslip (bulb). 4 *Gladiolus* x *colvillei* (corm). 5 Anemone (corm). 6 Ixia (bulb). 7 Bluebell (bulb). 8 Freesia (corm). 9 Dutch iris (bulb). 10 Watsonia (corm). 11 Hyacinth (bulb). 12 Tulip (bulb). 13 Snowflake (bulb). 14 Daffodil (bulb).

Tuberous roots are similar to tubers, but are modified roots, not stems, and grow in clusters from the stem base. Individual tubers can be separated with a small section of the old stem attached. Each tuber must have an "eye" to produce new plants (as with dahlias).

Pseudobulbs are fleshy, bulb-like swellings at a stem base, usually of specific species of orchid.

Planting bulbs

The requirements are not all the same for every bulb, and although we may have indicated some preferences within the A to Z plant entries, your final guide should be local information provided when you purchase bulbs.

To grow bulbs successfully, you must prepare the soil appropriately and provide good drainage, which is essential for most types even if they need moist soil; a few enjoy damper conditions. Most bulbs benefit from the addition of well-rotted compost or organic matter before planting time; this will also assist in better drainage. Unless the recommendations state otherwise, incorporate into the soil a small quantity of slow-release "bulb food" or a complete fertilizer, ensuring the bulbs don't come into direct contact with it. Where necessary, apply lime to neutralize acidic soils, or dolomite to break down heavy clay soils. To improve the drainage, you can also add sharp sand or gravel, construct raised beds, incorporate a drainage system or grow bulbs in containers.

Planting depths for bulbs & corms

A general guide for bulbs and corms is to plant to a depth 2–3 times their height. In this way, smaller bulbs are normally planted more shallowly to conserve their energy. Deep planting is recommended for many tall-growing varieties to provide extra support as well as protection from predators. In colder climates, deeper planting will help protect against the damage caused by severe freezing or cold snaps; in warmer locations, it will assist with loss of moisture during times of increased heat. In sandy soils, deeper planting is also often recommended. A few bulbs need to be planted with their necks at or just below the soil level (see the A to Z plant entry details).

Rhizomes, tubers, and pseudobulbs generally require shallow planting so new shoots are at or just below soil level.

How to plant bulbs

When planting bulbs into the garden, follow these step-by-step instructions.

1 Dig a hole for each bulb, allowing the appropriate depth for each. For single plantings or groupings use a small trowel as shown, or insert a cylindrical bulb-planting tool that extracts soil when it is removed (see photo 2 on page 469). For mass planting, digging a trench may be easier; it will also ensure the bulbs are planted to a uniform depth.

2 Position each bulb with the pointed end facing up, as it's from this part that new growth will emerge. There are a few exceptions, such as ranunculus—the "claws" are planted downwards. Plant the bulb firmly in the soil, avoiding any air pockets.

3 Backfill the hole with garden soil and apply a layer of mulch to conserve moisture, protect from temperature fluctuations, and reduce weed growth. Water thoroughly.

4 Insert a marker to indicate where the bulbs are planted. Or for accurate reference, label with its botanic, variety or common name.

When to plant bulbs

The following is a general guide; we have indicated some anomalies in our A to Z plant entries. If you are uncertain, refer to the information on bulb packs or on the cultural information leaflets that may accompany them.

Bulbs are usually purchased in their dormant state and need to be planted as soon as possible. They should not be left so that they dry out or buds shoot prematurely.

Plant hardy spring- and summer-flowering bulbs in the fall, once soil temperatures fall to a consistently cool temperature of 60°F (16°C), allowing them to develop roots and to satisfy the cold requirement of each species. In cold locations, plant bulbs six weeks before the ground freezes. Check the exact timings dictated by your local climate zone.

Plant tender bulbs (that can't withstand cold temperatures or frost) and summer-flowering bulbs in early spring, once the soil has warmed and the last frost has passed. Often these are treated as annuals.

Fall-flowering bulbs should be in the ground by late summer.

Chilling bulbs

In order to imitate their naturally cold, dormant environment, you can grow some bulbs outside their optimum climatic range by "chilling" them. Place selected species or varieties of plants such as hyacinths, tulips, and daffodils in labelled paper bags or nets in the crisper part of the refrigerator for approximately 6–12 weeks. Having been fooled into experiencing a "cold spell," they will come out of their dormant state to produce roots and buds once planted out into warmer temperatures.

Bulb maintenance

Once bulbs are established, little maintenance is required. Water well during growth stages and apply a regular liquid feed with a water-soluble fertilizer. Keep watering until the foliage has turned yellow, as bulbs replenish their energy reserves through photosynthesis to carry them through until the next growing season. This energy also produces new bulblets or cormlets. Once the leaves have yellowed and withered, watering should be withheld (but evergreen bulbs still require some moisture during dormancy).

Lifting, separating, & storing

Bulbs are lifted for storage if they're not frost-hardy. Lifting also reduces the likelihood of overcrowding.

Hardy bulbs can overwinter in the ground, but in frost-prone areas most half-hardy and tender bulbs will need to be lifted before or just after the first frost. Some can be left *in situ* with a thick layer of mulch applied for protection; others resent being disturbed, so check each plant's requirements.

As bulbs multiply within a garden bed, they get congested, competing for nutrients, water, and space. Generally they need dividing every 3–5 years. Those planted and left to naturalize are usually in a large area where lifting is seldom necessary or even possible, due to the sheer effort required.

1 Using a sharp spade, dig up bulbs when dormant, taking care not to cause injury. Remove any excess soil, but do not wash the bulbs.

2 Discard damaged bulbs or those showing signs of rot. Retaining the largest and healthiest bulbs, divide clumps with bulblets or cormlets into smaller clumps for planting later in the garden or in containers, giving away or discarding any leftovers.

3 Leave the bulbs in a well-ventilated, shady place and allow them to dry for a few days.

4 Remove the yellowed foliage and stems, leaving 2 in (5 cm) attached. Dust with a fungicidal powder to prevent rot. Most bulbs can be placed in shallow wooden trays, wire-netting trays, nylon stocking bags or unsealed paper bags in a cool, dry, well-ventilated position. Others prefer a packing medium such as sand, vermiculite or peat moss, or they may need warmer temperatures. Store until their normal planting time.

The natural look

If you want to create a casual effect, try naturalizing bulbs. This simply means that once you have planted bulbs en masse, leave them to their own devices and your garden won't have a manicured, tended look—it should

look more like a meadow. Some bulbs suitable for naturalizing enjoy the dappled light cast by deciduous trees just before or as they're producing new leaves, while others will happily grow in full sun. Rock gardens or garden beds might be better for smaller bulbs and those needing containing.

Large gardens look enticing with a wild, woodland area, and even small spaces can still accommodate drifts or clumps of flowers, offering a less formal, stilted look where bulbs can be planted close together. For the best effect, choose only the same variety (or two) rather than a mix, and plant in odd numbers. As with flower arranging and interior design, most objects and plants look better arranged in groups of odd numbers. However, don't choose an area where you're tempted to mow before the bulb foliage has yellowed and died down, as this will only stunt the following year's growth.

If you're growing bulbs within a grassy area, choose plants for their height so they're not obscured later when they're in flower and the grass is growing. Mow the lawn in the fall before planting, and if necessary, hand cut around bulb foliage to keep grass levels low when their growth starts. This may be the only option, especially in warmer climates where grass isn't dormant, as it may smother the bulbs and compete for nutrients.

The best bulbs to plant en masse are hardy, cold-climate species and varieties that multiply readily and rapidly. For spring flowers, choose crocus, daffodils, bluebell or grape hyacinth. Hyacinth will naturalize but can often look artificial, so are best planted selectively by incorporating them with softer-looking plants. Avoid planting hyacinth in regimented rows. For autumn blooms, try colchicum, sternbergia or cyclamen tucked into semishady spots beneath the canopy of deciduous trees or in a rock garden. In warmer climates, try varieties of daylilies, iris, freesias, sparaxis or ornithogalum in drifts or garden beds.

When "meadow" planting, randomly plant bulbs (see "How to plant bulbs" on page 459) for an informal effect, or plan your design with soft, sweeping drifts or large clumps. In a lawn area, a rectangle of turf will need to be dug and rolled away. Dig the soil out to a depth of about 1 ft (30 cm) and replace it with the existing soil, mixed with organic matter and slow-release fertilizer, to the depth that the base of your chosen bulbs need. Plant the bulbs randomly, then cover them with the soil mix to the original level. Water well, replace the turf, and water again.

Annuals, too, can be used for the meadow garden. Poppies, bachelor's buttons, California poppies, various daisies, evening primrose and others can be combined to look natural and uncontrived. Many of them will self-seed and reappear year after year.

Some bulbs naturalize readily and some annuals produce seed freely, so what may be considered part of a delightful garden display can turn into an environmental weed if planted in an inappropriate location or left unchecked. We have included plants like freesias that make some gardeners drool and others swear, so seek local advice if you're in doubt.

1 To achieve a natural effect, scatter a handful of bulbs where you want to plant them.

2 Twist the bulb planter into the ground to the correct depth, and pull it out again, still twisting.

3 Place the bulb in the hole in an upright position.

4 Replace some of the plug around the bulb until the top is level. Press into place.

"Forcing" bulbs for indoor display

You needn't be without colorful blooms during the cold winter months— create your own indoor display. "Forcing" is a term given to plants manipulated into blooming at a time when they would normally be dormant. Forced bulbs are ideal for northern hemisphere Christmas gifts and festive arrangements, or for early indoor, spring-flowering displays.

While not all bulbs lend themselves to this practice, some are tried and tested, and often these bulbs have a heady perfume. Strong-performing cool or cold-climate bulbs include selected species and varieties of daffodils, crocus, and tulips. Try others, such as lily-of-the-valley, grape hyacinth, snowdrop and squills, and check the specific requirements of each bulb when you purchase them.

One of the most popular and easiest plants for forcing is the large, fragrant Dutch hyacinth. They are commonly prepared by suppliers for forcing, and are the most successful early bloomers. For the best flowering display, plant bulbs crowded together, but not touching, in a shallow decorative pot or bowl.

Plant bulbs as soon as possible in a quality bulb-planting medium, with their necks at or just above soil level and their tips at the container's rim level. Water and place in a cool, dark place such as a cupboard, garage, shed, greenhouse or cold frame for 3–4 months. Keep moist, and once the shoots have reached approximately 2 in (5 cm) in height, gradually bring the pots out into the warmth and light.

Bulbs for forcing need to go through a chilling period, and if your storage spot isn't below 48°F (9°C) and above freezing, you will need to place the prepared pot into the refrigerator to allow for root formation. Keep moist but not wet, and avoid storing ripening fruit that may emit ethylene gas and prevent the flowers from blooming. At the time of purchase, check the chilling temperatures and duration required.

Hyacinths may also be grown in a "hyacinth glass," with the lower quarter of the bulb sitting in water. Keep in a cool spot as for other forced bulbs, and once the roots have formed well and the tip is showing growth, move it into a lighter, warmer position for flowering.

For prolonged blooming, keep plants out of direct sunlight, away from sources of heat, and by cool windowsills at night. After flowering, discard the bulbs, as they won't usually perform well in subsequent years.

Warmer climate bulbs that suit forcing and benefit from night-time temperatures of 55–63°F (13–17°C) are the popular and striking hippeastrum, the white *Lilium longiflorum*, and colorful Asiatic and Oriental lily hybrids. Some narcissus, such as *Narcissus tazetta* or paperwhites, bloom successfully, as do the easy-to-grow autumn crocus (*Colchicum autumnale*) and chincherinchee.

Enjoying a warm environment of around 65–70°F (18–21°C) in a sunny situation, these bulbs will flower indoors within about 6–10 weeks of being purchased and potted up. Plant bulbs with one-third showing above the potting medium level and water well. Some bulbs will need to be discarded after flowering; amaryllis, however, can be left in pots for repeat forcing, or in suitable locations, planted outdoors.

If you simply want to effortlessly enjoy bulbs indoors, potted, mini-garden displays can also be purchased pre-chilled and ready to bloom!

PESTS & DISEASES

We haven't put much emphasis on pests and diseases in this publication. That's because we want to inspire rather than worry you. Gardening is all about getting out there and having a go. Everything might be plain sailing with no problems, but if you do encounter some—well, it's easy to seek advice from books, garden centers or the Internet.

Because the growing season for annuals is relatively short, they don't attract a host of pests and diseases, and bulbs are much easier to care for than you might imagine too. The most important thing to remember is that the sounder your soil preparation and growing methods, the healthier your plants will be. And, of course, it's important to grow the right plant in the right place. Gardeners love to break this rule: those in warm climates long to grow those gorgeous cool-climate plants such as delphiniums and daffodils, while cool-climate gardeners like nothing better than the challenge of growing a tropical plant. But in fact it rarely works. Take a plant out of its natural climatic zone, grow a sun-loving plant in the shade, and you are likely to get weak, spindly results. And it is these plants that suffer most from pests and diseases.

Good soil, correct plant spacing to allow for air circulation, and regular deep watering will keep plants growing strongly as well as help prevent pests and diseases. Avoid bulb rot by providing good drainage. Prevent fungal diseases such as powdery mildew, rust, and leaf spots by avoiding watering late in the day. Rust on annuals such as calendula, hollyhocks, and snapdragons can be a problem. Remove the affected leaves, and avoid growing them in the same place two years in a row. Snails and slugs often love fleshy, strappy-leaved bulbs and seedlings; caterpillars and cutworms can affect plants too. Prevention is much easier than cure.

Snail and slug pellets do the job, but some are more pet-friendly than others, so check the packet if this is an issue, or place them inside a lidded margarine container. Punch holes in the lid so that snails can get in to eat the pellets but the dog (or children) can't. An alternative is to use a beer or bran trap. Place some bran on top of a container filled with water or just fill it with beer; bury the container until the rim is at soil level. Snails will try and eat the bran or drink the beer and drown.

We haven't recommended chemical treatments for any pests and diseases, as not only are these best avoided but also the products available vary from country to country.

GLOSSARY

ACID SOIL: soil that has a ph of less than 7 or that is lacking in lime.

ALKALINE SOIL: soil that has a ph of more than 7 or that is lime-rich.

ANNUAL: a plant with a natural life cycle of one season, usually within a year.

ANTHER: the pollen-bearing portion of the stamen.

AXIL: the part of the plant where the leaf joins the stem.

BASAL: at the base of an organ or structure.

BEDDING PLANT: a plant that is often mass planted for a temporary garden display.

BIENNIAL: a plant that has a natural life cycle of two years.

BRACT: a modified leaf directly behind a flower or cluster of flowers; sometimes brightly colored.

CALYX (pl. CALYCES): the outer part of a flower; it consists of sepals and may be brightly colored or decorative.

COROLLA: the part of a flower that is formed by the petals.

CORONA: a crown- or cup-like appendage or ring of appendages within the center of the flower.

CROWN: the plant part where the stems meet the soil; new shoots grow from the top of the crown, roots from the bottom. Also the top of the tree, formed by the canopy.

CULTIVAR: a contraction of "cultivated variety." A distinct form of a plant with at least one different feature from the species; usually a result of selected breeding programs or cultivation.

CUTTING: a section of leaf, stem or root that is separated from a plant in order to reproduce it.

DEAD-HEADING: the removal of finished flowers in order to prevent seeds from forming and to encourage the production of new blooms.

DECIDUOUS PLANT: a plant that loses its leaves annually and

becomes dormant as part of its natural life cycle.

DISC FLORET: a small, often inconspicuous flower, frequently making up the central portion of a flower head.

DIVISION: a method of propagation whereby a plant clump is divided into smaller sections.

DOUBLE FLOWER: a flower that has two or more times as many petals than the usual number in the species.

EVERGREEN: a plant that retains its leaves throughout the year.

FAMILY: a group of related plants, including genera and species.

FILAMENT: the slender part of a stamen that supports the anther.

FLORET: a single flower in a composite arrangement, or head of many flowers.

FULL SUN: at least six hours of unfiltered sun per day.

GENUS (pl. GENERA): a category in plant classification, consisting of a single species or a group of related species.

HABIT: the plant's usual form, appearance, and way of growing.

HALF-HARDY: can withstand temperatures down to 32°F (0°C).

HARDY: can withstand temperatures down to 5°F (−15°C). In warm climates, "hardy" is often used colloquially to indicate plants that will tolerate high temperatures and/or dry conditions.

HERBACEOUS: plants that die down at the end of the growing season.

HYBRID: a plant that is the result of crossing different genera, species or cultivars.

IN SITU: to sow seed directly into the garden where plants are to grow.

INFLORESCENCE: a flowering stem with more than one flower.

MULCH: a layer of material applied to the soil around plants to conserve moisture and aid weed control. May be organic—for example, compost and manure—or inorganic—for example, pebbles.

PART SHADE: unfiltered morning sun but shade in the afternoon; or moderately shady throughout the day.

PERENNIAL: a plant that lives for at least three years; in gardens, the term mostly applies to non-woody plants, but can also describe the habits of shrubs and trees.

RACEME: an unbranched flowering stem of stalked flowers, with the youngest at the top.

SCAPE: a leafless flower stem arising from a foliage clump.

SELF SEED (SELF SOW): to release viable seed that germinates and grows around the parent plant.

SEMI-EVERGREEN: plants that retain some leaves, or lose older ones only when new growth is produced.

SEPAL: a petal-like structure that forms part of the calyx.

SERIES (also STRAIN): a group of cultivars of annuals that share most of the same characteristics, but differ from one another by one characteristic, usually color.

SPECIES: the basic unit of plant classification, consisting of very closely related plants within a genus; abbreviated to "sp." (singular) or "spp." (plural).

STAMEN: in a flower, the pollen-producing, male reproductive organ, comprising a filament and an anther.

SUBSHRUB: woody-based plant with soft, usually herbaceous stems.

TENDER: a plant vulnerable to frost damage.

TERMINAL: located at the end of a shoot or stem.

UMBEL: a flat or rounded inflorescence with the flower stems arising from one point.

VARIEGATED: irregular coloring; a leaf that is naturally green but displays other colors.

VARIETY: technically, a plant that has at least one different feature from the species generally occurring naturally, but the term is often loosely used to describe plants that have been bred or selected.

WHORL: a circular arrangement of three or more leaves or flowers arising from a single point on the stem.

INDEX

This index includes an index of common names.

PHOTO CREDITS

The publisher would like to thank Judy Horton and Arthur Yates & Co Limited, and Oasis for supplying color transparencies for this book.

The publisher would also like to thank the following for allowing photography in their gardens:

Sally Allison, 'Lyddington', North Canterbury, New Zealand: 29.
'Ashfield' Sandy Bay, Hobart TAS: 267.
Sarah Baker, Leichardt NSW: 371.
Bankstown Municipal Park, Bankstown NSW: 126, 226, 311, 337.
Barkers Nursery, Turramurra NSW: 8.
A G & L A Barrett, 'Nooroo', Mt Wilson NSW: 446.
G Boots, ACT: 379.
'Bringalbit', Sidonia VIC: 322, 345, 402–3.
Brisbane Botanic Gardens, Mt Coot-tha QLD: 232.
'Buskers End', Bowral NSW: 240.
Mr and Mrs Andrew Cannon, Manildra NSW: 279.
Heather Cant, Burradoo NSW: 169, 201, 349.
Castle Hill Park, Castle Hill NSW: 186.
Fay Cavenett, Huonville TAS: 223 (R), 302.
Centennial Park, Sydney NSW: 331.
'Cheplaknet', Moss Vale NSW: 474.
'Cherry Cottage', Mt Wilson NSW: 359.
Colorwise Nursery: 293.
'Convent Gallery', Daylesford VIC: 262–3.
Cooramilla Nursery, Browns Creek NSW: 120, 274.

E Cossil and T Carlstrom, Frenchs Forest NSW: 306.
'Craigie Lea', Leura NSW: 237.
Dr G Cummins, Pymble NSW: 430.
'Curry Flat', Nimmitabel NSW: 391.
'Dunrath', West Pennant Hills NSW: 130.
Zeny Edwards, Turramurra NSW: 12.
'Eryldene', Gordon NSW: 304, 429.
'Everglades', Leura NSW: 466.
'Ewanrigg', Leura NSW: 144 (bottom L), 146–7, 151.
J & J Ferris, Longueville NSW: 419.
Floriade, Canberra ACT: 6–7, 88, 144 (top L), 148 (bottom R), 149, 150 (R), 378.
'Foxglove Spires', Tilba Tilba NSW: 30, 281, 297.
DD Franklin: 90, 285.
J Hancock, Erskineville NSW: 250.
Harvey Garden, Gravelly Beach TAS: 254–5, 258, 407.
The Hedgerow Roses, Tumbarumba NSW: 198.
'Heronswood', Dromana VIC: 18–19, 156, 197, 298.
Diana Hill, Ashfield NSW: 33, 84 (top R), 85.
'Hillview', Exeter NSW: 87, 97, 148 (top R), 182–3, 223 (L), 241, 383, 462.
Mrs Hilyard, Canberra ACT: 148 (top L).
'Jarra Farm', Barkers Creek VIC: 261, 329.
'Kennerton Green', Mittagong NSW: 11, 91, 101, 148 (bottom L), 256–7, 288, 303, 357, 404–5.
'Kiah Park', Jaspers Brush NSW: 86, 313.
Meredith Kirton, Putney NSW: 65.
P & S Lawrence, Hunterville New Zealand: 277.
Lawrences Nursery, Mirboo VIC: 386.
Chris Leal, Turramurra NSW: 234.

Published in 2004 by Bay Books, an imprint of Murdoch Magazines Pty Ltd
©Text, design and commissioned photographs copyright Murdoch Books® 2004

Printed by Midas Printing (Asia) Ltd
PRINTED IN CHINA

Chief Executive: Juliet Rogers
Publisher: Kay Scarlett

Editor: Sarah Baker
Designer: Michelle Cutler
Design Concept: Marylouise Brammer
Creative Director: Marylouise Brammer
Editorial Director: Diana Hill
Production: Monika Paratore